Heirloom Afghans™

the Needlecraft Shop®

Heirloom Afghans™

EDITOR Judy Crow
ART DIRECTOR Brad Snow
PUBLISHING SERVICES DIRECTOR Brenda Gallmeyer

ASSISTANT EDITOR Carol Alexander
ASSISTANT ART DIRECTOR Nick Pierce
COPY SUPERVISOR Michelle Beck
COPY EDITORS Susanna Tobias, Marcia VanGelder,
 Judy Weatherford
TECHNICAL EDITOR Mary Ann Frits
TECHNICAL ARTIST Nicole Gage

GRAPHIC ARTS SUPERVISOR Ronda Bechinski
GRAPHIC ARTISTS Vicki Staggs, Jessi Butler
PRODUCTION ASSISTANTS Marj Morgan,
 Judy Neuenschwander

PHOTOGRAPHY SUPERVISOR Tammy Christian
PHOTOGRAPHY Matthew Owen
PHOTOGRAPHY ASSISTANT Tammy Steiner

First Printing: 2008, China
Library of Congress Control Number: 2007940896
Hardcover ISBN: 978-1-57367-307-5
Softcover ISBN: 978-1-57367-318-1

Every effort has been made to ensure the accuracy and completeness
of the instructions in this book. However, we cannot be responsible for
human error or for the results when using materials other than those
specified in the instructions, or for variations in individual work.

DRGbooks.com

1 2 3 4 5 6 7 8 9

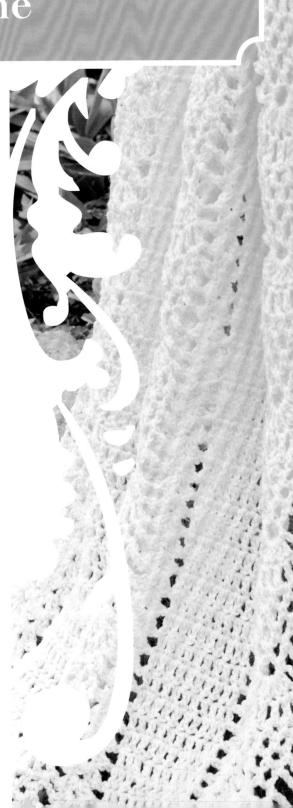

Welcome

Inspiration is a wonderful feeling! And when I'm inspired about something new and exciting, I just can't wait to share it with all my friends. Within the pages you will find a treasure of original creations from the world's premier afghan designers. From classic favorites transformed into new through different techniques and stitches, to breathtaking vibrant jewel tone styles, this collection is a must for every crocheter.

Drift away in remembrances of childhood ventures as you wrap yourself in an afghan from our Old-Time Pineapples and Filets chapter, or see Mother Nature at her finest in our Vintage Florals. Find peaceful solitude among the folds of our stately designs stitched in an opulent array of Jewel Tones or see how the old and new collide with magical precision in the renditions of our Forever Quilts chapter.

Like the afghans we crochet, the everyday moments we share with family and friends are remembered in skeins and stitches. May you fondly remember the past as you warmly embrace the future with this selection of afghans that are sure to warm your hearts as well as your toes!

Warm Stitching,

Contents

Legacy Lace

The great writers of the past used ink and paper to capture the times of their lives, leaving a legacy that has endured for generations in the form of poetry and prose. Penned with hook and yarn instead, crochet offers that same lasting heritage for your family for years to come.

Pearls & Lace

Design by Rhonda Dodds

SKILL LEVEL
 INTERMEDIATE

FINISHED SIZE
53 x 56 inches

MATERIALS
- Red Heart Super Saver medium (worsted) weight yarn (7 oz/ 364 yds/198g per skein):
    7 skeins #334 buff
    2 skeins #316 soft white
- Brown Sheep Lamb's Pride medium (worsted) weight yarn (4 oz/190 yds/ 113g per skein):
    1 skein #M69 old sage
- Sizes H/8/5mm and J/10/6mm crochet hooks or size needed to obtain gauge
- Tapestry needle
- Sewing needle
- 6mm white pearls: 472
- Dark sewing thread
- Stitch markers

GAUGE
Size H hook: [Sk next 2 chs, V-st in next ch] 3 times = 4 inches; 4 rows = 3 inches

PATTERN NOTES
Weave in ends as work progresses.

Join rounds with a slip stitch unless otherwise stated.

Chain-3 at beginning of double crochet rows counts as first double crochet unless otherwise stated.

SPECIAL STITCHES
V-stitch (V-st): (Dc, ch 2, dc) in place indicated.
Double V-stitch (double V-st): (2 dc, ch 2, 2 dc) in place indicated.
Bead single crochet (bead sc): Insert hook in indicated st, yo, draw lp through, slide bead up to hook, yo and draw through 2 lps on hook.

INSTRUCTIONS

AFGHAN
Body
Row 1 (WS): With size J hook and buff, ch 124, change to size H hook, **V-st** *(see Special Stitches)* in 5th ch from hook *(beg 4 sk chs count as a dc),* *sk next 2 chs, V-st in next ch, rep from * across to last 2 chs, sk next ch, dc in last ch, turn. *(40 V-sts, 2 dc)*
Row 2 (RS): Ch 3 *(see Pattern Notes),* **double V-st** *(see Special Stitches)* in ch-2 sp of each V-st across, dc in 4th ch of beg 4 sk chs, turn. *(40 double V-sts)*
Row 3: Ch 3, V-st in ch-2 sp of each double V-st across, dc in 3rd ch of beg ch-3, turn.
Row 4: Ch 3, double V-st in ch-2 sp of each V-st across, dc in 3rd ch of beg ch-3, turn. *(40 double V-sts)*
Rows 5–74: [Rep rows 3 and 4 alternately] 35 times.
Row 75: Rep row 3. **Do not fasten off.**

Continued on page 25

Amanda Whorl

Design by Rosalie Johnston

SKILL LEVEL

 EXPERIENCED

FINISHED SIZE

48 x 56 inches

MATERIALS

- Red Heart Super Saver medium (worsted) weight yarn (7 oz/ 364 yds/198g per skein):
    4 skeins #382 country blue
- Size I/9/5.5mm crochet hook or size needed to obtain gauge
- Tapestry needle

GAUGE

4 tr = 1 inch

PATTERN NOTES

Weave in ends as work progresses.

Join rounds with a slip stitch unless otherwise stated.

Chain-4 at beginning of treble crochet rows counts as first treble crochet unless otherwise stated.

SPECIAL STITCHES

Picot: Ch 5, sl st in 5th ch from hook.
Small picot: Ch 3, sl st in indicated st.

INSTRUCTIONS

FIRST LARGE MOTIF
First Segment
Row 1 (RS): Ch 12, join with sl st in first ch to form a ring, **ch 4** *(see Pattern Notes),* [tr in ring, ch 6, dc in top of last tr, tr in ring] 3 times, tr in ring, ch 2, 9 tr in ring, turn. *(17 tr, 3 ch-6 sps, 1 ch-2 sp)*
Row 2: Picot *(see Special Stitches),* sk first tr, sc in each of next 8 tr, leaving rem sts unworked, turn.
Row 3: Ch 1, sc in first sc, ch 3, sk next 3 sc, sc in next sc, leaving rem sts unworked, turn.
Row 4: Ch 9, sk first sc, sk next ch-3 sp, sl st in next sc, turn.

2nd Segment
Row 1 (RS): Ch 4, [tr in ch-9 sp, ch 6, dc in top of last tr, tr in ch-9 sp] 3 times, tr in same sp, ch 2, 9 tr in same sp, ch 2, sc in picot of previous segment, turn. *(17 tr, 1 sc, 3 ch-6 sps, 2 ch-2 sps)*
Row 2: Small picot *(see Special Stitches)* in first tr, sc in each of next 8 tr, turn.
Row 3: Ch 1, sc in first sc, ch 3, sk next 3 sc, sc in next sc, leaving rem sts unworked, turn.
Row 4: Ch 9, sk first sc, sk next ch-3 sp, sl st in next sc, turn.

3rd through 7th Segments
Work same as 2nd Segment.

8th Segment

Row 1 (RS): Ch 4, [tr in ch-9 sp, ch 6, dc in top of last tr, tr in ch-9 sp] 3 times, tr in same sp, ch 2, 9 tr in same sp, ch 2, sc in picot of 7th Segment, ch 1, sc in picot of First Segment, turn. *(17 tr, 1 sc, 3 ch-6 sps, 2 ch-2 sps, 1 ch-1 sp)*

Row 2: Small picot in first tr, sc in each of next 4 tr, sl st in ring of First Segment, sc in each of next 4 tr, sl st in ring of First Segment. Fasten off.

Center Ring

With RS facing, work inside around center of Motif by joining yarn with sl st in side of any sc, ch 1, sc in same sp, [sc in next picot, sc in side of next sc] 7 times, sc in next picot, join in beg sc. Fasten off.

Edging

Rnd 1: *Join* yarn in any ch-6 sp on any Large Motif, ch 1, sc in same sp, *ch 5, sc in next ch-6 sp, rep from * 23 times, ch 3, join with dc in first sc *(joining dc counts as a ch-5 sp). (24 ch-5 sps)*

Rnd 2: *Ch 7, sc in next ch-5 sp, rep from * 23 times, ch 4, join with tr in joining dc *(joining tr counts as a ch-7 sp). Fasten off. (24 ch-7 sps)*

2ND–18TH LARGE MOTIFS

Work same as First Large Motif through rnd 1 of Edging. Join Motifs to previous Motifs by working either a 1-sided joining rnd 2 or a 2-sided joining rnd 2 as necessary to have 3 strips of 4 Motifs each and 2 strips of 3 Motifs each.

Rnd 2 (one-sided joining): *Ch 7, sc in next ch-5 sp, rep from * 23 times, ch 4, join with tr in joining dc *(joining tr counts as a ch-7 sp). Fasten off. (24 ch-7 sps)*

Rnd 2 (two-sided joining): *Ch 7, sc in next ch-5 sp, rep from * 14 times, ch 4, sc in any ch-7 sp of previous motif, **ch 3, sc in next ch-7 sp on opposite motif, rep from * 8 times, ch 4, sc in next ch-7 sp on opposite motif. Fasten off.

Note: Six top ch-7 sps are skipped and 6 side ch-7 sps are used for side-to-side joining. Six unused ch-7 sps should be at bottom of motif. Motifs should form a straight line.

Amanda Whorl
Diagram 1
Join yarn at point A. Work joining to point B.

STRIP JOINING

Note: On far right motif of strip of 4 motifs, mark 4th ch-7 sp to right of joining mesh, at bottom of motif (see A on Diagram 1). On far left motif, mark 4th ch-7 sp to left of joining mesh at bottom of motif (see B on Diagram 1). Center 3-motif strip under 4-motif strip, as shown in Diagram 1.

Join yarn in marked ch-7 sp on right-hand side, ch 1, sc in same ch-7 sp, ch 4, sc in adjacent ch-7 sp on 3-motif strip below, ch 3, sc in next ch-7 sp on 4-motif strip, ch 3, sc in next ch-7 sp on 3-motif strip. When joining through area of side-to-side meshwork, sc in sc, rather than in ch-5 sps. Continue with (ch 3, sc) zigzag joining across, (ch 4, sc) in marked ch-7 sp on left. Fasten off.

To join next 4-motif strip, center it under previously joined 3-motif strip. Mark 4th ch-7 sp to right of joining mesh at top of far right motif of 4-motif strip. Mark 4th ch-7 sp to left of joining mesh at top of far left motif of 4-motif strip. Join yarn in marked ch-7 sp on right, ch 1, sc in same ch-7 sp, ch 4, sc in adjacent ch-7 sp on 3-motif strip above, continue with (ch 3, sc) zigzag joining across as described above, (ch 4, sc) in marked ch-7 sp on left. Fasten off.

Referring to Diagram 2, rep joining for all 5 horizontal strips.

Amanda Whorl
Diagram 2

BORDER

Hold piece with 1 short end at top, join yarn around corner ch-7 sp, ch 1, sc in same sp, *ch 7, sc in next ch-7 sp, rep from * across first motif to side-to-side joining mesh, **(Note: work following short rows to fill in indentation)*, [ch 7, sc in next ch sp] 3 times across mesh, ch 4, tr in first ch-7 sp on next motif, turn, [ch 7, sc in next ch-7 sp] 3 times, ch 4, tr in next ch-7 sp, turn, (ch 7, sc in next ch-7 sp) across mesh to end of next motif, rep from ** twice, working across next side, ***(ch 7, sc in next ch-7 sp) down side of top motif and bottom of top left motif, at mesh area (between motifs), work (ch-7 sp, sc) in sc in mesh, (ch 7, sc in next ch-7 sp) across left side of motif in next row, in mesh area, (ch-7 sp, sc) in sc, (ch 7, sc in next ch-7 sp) across top of motif in next row, rep from *** down left side of afghan, work across bottom same as top, work across right side of afghan same as left side, join in beg sc. Fasten off.

SMALL MOTIF

Make 4.

Note: Small Motif is one segment of Large Motif. Make 1 Small Motif at a time. Join each Small Motif to afghan as it is made. Join to afghan after it is made; then make next one.

Rnd 1: Ch 12, join with sl st in first ch to form a ring, ch 4, [tr in ring, ch 6, dc in top of last tr, tr in ring] 3 times, tr in ring, ch 2, 9 tr in ring. **Do not turn.**

Rnd 2: Ch 7, [sc in next ch-6 sp, ch 7] 3 times, sc in next ch-2 sp, ch 7, sk next 4 tr, sc in next tr, ch 7, sk next 3 tr, join in last tr.

Rnd 3: *[Sc, ch 6] twice in next ch-7 sp, rep from * 4 times, (sc, ch 6, sc) in next ch-7 sp, ch 3, join with tr in beg sc.

Rnd 4: *Ch 7, sc in next ch-6 sp, rep from * around, ch 4, join with tr in joining tr.

Rnd 5: *Ch 7, sc in next ch-7 sp, rep from * around, ch 4, join with tr in joining tr.

Rnd 6: *Ch 8, sc in next ch-7 sp, rep from * around, ch 5, join with tr in joining tr.

Note: Place Small Motif in area of indentation at edge of afghan (see Diagram 3); position motif with 3 ch-6 sps of rnd 1 on top and to right.

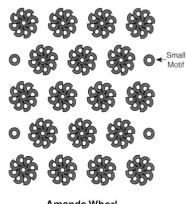

Amanda Whorl
Diagram 3

← Small Motif

Place outer edge of motif even with outer edge of afghan. Follow same placement directions for both right and left sides of afghan.

Rnd 7: Ch 7, sc in ch-7 sp of afghan directly below Small Motif, ch 5, sc in same sp of Small Motif, ch 3, sc in next ch-7 sp on afghan, ch 3, sc in next ch-8 sp of Small Motif, continue around with (ch 3, sc) zigzag joining to last 2 sps, ch 5, sc in next sp, ch 7, sc in last sp. Fasten off.

OUTER BORDER

Join yarn in ch-7 sp at right upper corner of afghan, ch 1, (sc, ch 1, hdc, ch 4, 2 hdc) in same sp, picot sc in next sc, *(2 hdc, ch 4, hdc) in next ch-7 sp, sc in next sc, (hdc, ch 4, 2 hdc) in next ch-7 sp, picot, sc in next sc, rep from * around, join in first sc. Fasten off. ■

Lime Lace

Design by Christine L. Walter

SKILL LEVEL

 ■■■□ INTERMEDIATE

FINISHED SIZE

48 x 60 inches

MATERIALS

- Lion Brand Microspun light (light worsted) weight yarn (2½ oz/168 yds/70g per skein): 12 skeins #194 lime
- Size H/8/5mm crochet hook or size needed to obtain gauge
- Tapestry needle

GAUGE

12 sts = 4 inches; 8 rows = 4 inches

PATTERN NOTES

Weave in ends as work progresses.

Join rounds with a slip stitch unless otherwise stated.

Chain-3 at beginning of double crochet rows counts as first double crochet unless otherwise stated.

Chain-4 at beginning of double crochet rows counts as first double crochet and chain-1 space unless otherwise stated.

Chain-6 at beginning of double crochet rows counts as first double crochet and chain-3 space unless otherwise stated.

INSTRUCTIONS

CENTER

Row 1 (RS): Ch 173, 2 dc in 4th ch from hook *(beg 3 sk chs count as first dc)*, *ch 3, sk next 3 chs, sc in next ch, ch 3, sk next 3 chs, 2 dc in next ch, dc in next ch, 2 dc in next ch, rep from * 15 times, ch 3, sk next 3 chs, sc in next ch, ch 3, sk next 3 chs, 2 dc in next ch, dc in next ch, turn. *(86 dc, 17 sc, 34 ch-3 sps)*

Row 2: Ch 3 *(see Pattern Notes)*, dc in each of next 2 dc, *2 dc in next ch-3 sp, ch 1, 2 dc in next ch-3 sp, dc in each of next 5 dc, rep from * 15 times, 2 dc in next ch-3 sp, ch 1, 2 dc in next ch-3 sp, dc in each of next 2 dc, dc in 3rd ch of beg 3 sk chs, turn. *(154 dc, 17 ch-1 sps)*

Row 3: Ch 3, dc in each of next 2 dc, *ch 3, sc in next ch-1 sp, ch 3, sk next 2 dc **, dc in each of next 5 dc, rep from * across, ending last rep at **, dc in each of next 2 dc, dc in 3rd ch of beg ch-3, turn. *(86 dc, 17 sc, 34 ch-3 sps)*

Row 4: Ch 6 *(see Pattern Notes)*, *sc in next ch-3 sp, 5 dc in next sc, sc in next ch-3 sp, ch 3, sk next 2 dc **, dc in next dc, ch 3, rep from * across, ending last rep at **, dc in 3rd ch of beg ch-3, turn. *(103 dc, 34 sc, 34 ch-3 sps)*

Row 5: Ch 3, *2 dc in next ch-3 sp, ch 3, sk next sc, sk next 2 dc, sc in next dc, ch 3, 2 dc in next ch-3 sp **, dc in next dc, rep from * across, ending last rep at **, dc in 3rd ch of

Continued on page 25

Tree Blossoms

Design by Ruthie Marks

Design by Ruthie Marks

SKILL LEVEL
 INTERMEDIATE

FINISHED SIZE
39 x 56 inches

MATERIALS

- Red Heart Super Saver medium (worsted) weight yarn (7 oz/ 364 yds/198g per skein):
  4 skeins #372 rose pink
- Size H/8/5mm crochet hook or size needed to obtain gauge
- Tapestry needle

GAUGE
Tree trunk = 2 inches tall

PATTERN NOTES
Weave in ends as work progresses.

Join rounds with a slip stitch unless otherwise stated.

Chain-5 at beginning of treble crochet rows counts as first treble crochet and chain-1 space unless otherwise stated.

Chain-6 at beginning of double treble crochet rows counts as first double treble crochet and chain-1 space unless otherwise stated.

INSTRUCTIONS

AFGHAN
Body

Row 1 (RS): Ch 14, *sc in 2nd ch from hook, sc in each of next 5 chs, sl st in next ch, turn, sc in each of next 6 sc, ch 5, working in unused lps on opposite side of beg ch-14, sc in each of next 6 chs *(tree trunk)*, ch 19, rep from * 8 times, sc in 2nd ch from hook, sc in each of next 5 chs, sl st in next ch, turn, sc in each of next 6 sc, ch 5, working in unused lps on opposite side of beg ch-14, sc in each of next 6 chs *(tree trunk)*, turn. *(10 tree trunks)*

Row 2: Ch 7, sc in 2nd ch from hook, *ch 3, sk next 5 chs, sk next 3 sc, tr in next sc, ch 1, [tr, ch 1] 9 times in next ch-5 sp, sk next 2 sc, tr in next sc, ch 3, sk next 5 chs, sc in next sc, rep from * across, turn.

Row 3: Ch 6 *(see Pattern Notes)*, sk next 2 ch sps, *[sc in next ch-1 sp, ch 3] 8 times, sk next 4 ch sps, rep from * 8 times, [sc in next ch-1 sp, ch 3] 7 times, sc in next ch-1 sp, ch 1, sk next ch-1 sp, dtr in last sc, turn.

Row 4: Ch 15, sc in 5th ch from hook, sc in each of next 5 chs, *ch 5, sk next 3 ch-3 sps, sc in next ch-3 sp, ch 6, sk next 3 ch-3 sps, dtr in next ch-3 sp, ch 7, sc in 2nd ch from hook, sc in each of next 5 chs, turn, sl st in first ch of next ch-6 sp, turn, sc in each of next 6 sc, ch 5, working in unused lps on opposite side of ch-7, sc in each of next 6 chs *(tree trunk)*, rep from * 8 times,

Continued on page 26

Serene Meadow

Design by Lori Zeller

SKILL LEVEL
■■■□ EXPERIENCED

FINISHED SIZE
46 x 48 inches

MATERIALS
• Medium (worsted) weight yarn:
    16 oz/800 yds/453g aran
    6 oz/300 yds/170g each light green
    and medium green
    4 oz/200 yds/113g dark green

4 MEDIUM

• Size H/8/5mm crochet hook or size
  needed to obtain gauge
• Hairpin needle
• Tapestry needle
• Stitch markers

GAUGE
5 V-sts = 3½ inches
Motif = 23½ x 12 inches

PATTERN NOTES
Weave in ends as work progresses.

Join rounds with a slip stitch unless
otherwise stated.

Chain-4 at beginning of double crochet
rows/rounds counts as first double
crochet and chain-1 space unless
otherwise stated.

SPECIAL STITCHES
Shell: [Tr, ch 1] 4 times in indicated st or
sp, tr in same st or sp.

**Beginning double crochet shell (beg dc
shell):** Ch 4, [dc, ch 1] twice in indicated st
or sp, dc in same st or sp.
Double crochet shell (dc shell): [Dc, ch 1] 3
times in indicated st or sp, dc in same st or sp.
Beginning V-stitch (beg V-st): Ch 4, dc in
indicated st or sp.
V-stitch (V-st): (Dc, ch 1, dc) in indicated
st or sp.

HAIRPIN LACE TECHNIQUE
1. With loom set at 3 inches, make a long
slip knot equal to half of the width of the
loom; place slip knot on left prong.
2. Replace bottom crossbar.
3. Bring the yarn around the RS of the
loom to the back.
4. Insert hook through slip knot, yo and
draw lp through, ch 1.
5. Pass hook to back, between prongs, while
turning loom clockwise (right to left).
6. Insert hook through lp on left prong, yo
and draw lp through (2 lps on hook).

Hairpin Lace Illustration

1

3

2

4

7. Yo and draw through both lps.
Rep steps 5–7 for required number of lps on each prong.

INSTRUCTIONS

FIRST PANEL
First Motif

Row 1: With aran, work Hairpin Lace Technique until you have 45 lps on each prong.

Rnd 2: Now working in rnds, ch 6, **shell** *(see Special Stitches)* in 6th ch from hook *(beg 5 sk chs count as first tr and ch-1 sp)*, ch 1, shell in same ch, ch 1, [shell under next 5 lps of hairpin lace, sc under next 5 lps] 4 times, shell under next 5 lps, ch 1, shell in st at bottom tip of hairpin strip, ch 1, tr in same st, ch 1, [shell under next 5 lps of hairpin lace, sc under next 5 lps] 4 times, shell under next 5 lps, ch 1, **join** *(see Pattern Notes)* in 5th ch of beg ch-6. Fasten off. *(16 shells, 2 tr, 8 sc, 4 ch-1 sps)*

Rnd 3: Join light green with sc in first ch-1 sp on previous rnd, [ch 3, sc in next ch-1 sp] 4 times, ch 1, (dc, ch 2, dc) in next ch-1 sp, ch 1, [sc in next ch-1 sp, ch 3] 19 times, sc in next ch-1 sp, ch 1, (dc, ch 2, dc) in next ch-1 sp, ch 1, sc in next ch-1 sp, [ch 3, sc in next ch-1 sp] 4 times, ch 1, (dc, ch 2, dc) in next ch-1 sp, ch 1, [sc in next ch-1 sp, ch 3] 19 times, sc in next ch-1 sp, ch 1, (dc, ch 2, dc) in next ch-1 sp, ch 1, join in first sc. Fasten off. *(8 dc, 50 sc, 30 ch-3 sps, 4 ch-2 sps, 8 ch-1 sps)*

Rnd 4: Join medium green in last ch-2 sp made on previous rnd, **beg dc shell** *(see Special Stitches)* in same sp, *ch 2, [sc in next ch-3 sp, ch 3] 3 times, sc in next ch-2 sp, ch 2, **dc shell** *(see Special Stitches)* in next ch-2 sp, ch 2, [sc in next ch-3 sp, ch 3] 18 times, sc in next ch-3 sp, ch 2 **, dc shell in next ch-2 sp, rep from * once, ending rep at **, join in 3rd ch of beg ch-4. *(4 dc shells, 46 sc, 42 ch-3 sps, 8 ch-2 sps)*

Rnd 5: Sl st in next ch-1 sp, **beg V-st** *(see Special Stitches)* in same sp, (dc, ch 2, dc) in next ch-1 sp, **V-st** *(see Special Stitches)* in next ch-1 sp, *[ch 3, sc in next ch-3 sp] 3 times, ch 3, V-st in next ch-1 sp, (dc, ch 2, dc) in next ch-1 sp, V-st in next ch-1 sp, [ch 3, sc in next ch-3 sp] 18 times, ch 3 **, V-st in next ch-1 sp, (dc, ch 2, dc) in next ch-1 sp, V-st in next ch-1 sp, rep from * once, ending rep at **, join in 3rd ch of beg ch-4. Fasten off. *(8 V-sts, 8 dc, 42 sc, 46 ch-3 sps, 4 ch-2 sps)*

Rnd 6: Join dark green with sc in first ch-2 sp on previous rnd, ch 3, sc in same sp, *[ch 3, sc in next ch-space] 6 times, ch 3, (sc, ch 3, sc) in next ch-2 sp, [ch 3, sc in next ch sp] 21 times, ch 3 **, (sc, ch 3, sc) in next ch-3 sp, rep from * once, ending rep at **, join in first sc. Fasten off. *(62 sc, 62 ch-3 sps)*

Rnd 7: Join medium green in first ch-3 sp on previous rnd, beg dc shell in same sp, *ch 1, V-st in each of next 7 ch-3 sps, ch 1, dc shell in next ch-3 sp, ch 1, V-st in each of next 22 ch-3 sps, ch 1 **, dc shell in next ch-3 sp, rep from * once, ending rep at **, join in 3rd ch of beg ch-4. Fasten off. *(4 dc shells, 58 V-sts, 8 ch-1 sps)*

Rnd 8: Join light green with sc in first ch-1 sp of previous rnd, ch 5, sc in 5th ch from hook, sc in same sp, ch 1, dc shell in next ch-1 sp, ch 1, (sc, ch 5, sc in 5th ch from hook, sc) in next ch-1 sp, *(sc, ch 5, sc in 5th ch from hook, sc) in ch-1 sp of each of next 7 V-sts, sk next ch-1 sp, (sc, ch 5, sc in 5th ch from hook, sc) in next ch-1 sp, ch 1, dc shell in next ch-1 sp, ch 1, (sc, ch 5, sc in 5th ch from hook, sc) in next ch-1 sp, (sc, ch 5, sc in 5th ch from hook, sc) in ch-1 sp of each of next 22 V-sts, sk next ch-1 sp **, (sc, ch 5, sc in 5th ch from hook, sc) in next ch-1 sp, ch 1, dc shell in next ch-1 sp, ch 1, (sc, ch 5, sc in 5th ch from hook, sc) in next ch-1 sp, rep from * once, ending rep at **, join in beg sc. Fasten off. *(4 dc shells, 132 sc, 66 ch-5 sps, 8 ch-1 sps)*

Rnd 9: Join aran in first ch-1 sp of first dc shell on previous rnd, beg V-st in same sp, *(dc, ch 2, dc) in next ch-2 sp, V-st in next ch-1 sp, V-st in each of next 9 ch-5 sps, sk next ch-1 sp, V-st in next ch-1 sp, (dc, ch 2, dc) in next ch-2 sp, V-st in next ch-1 sp,

V-st in each of next 24 ch-5 sps **, sk next ch-1 sp, V-st in next ch-1 sp, rep from * once, ending rep at **, join in 3rd ch of beg ch-4. *(74 V-sts, 8 dc, 4 ch-2 sps)*

Rnd 10: Sl st in first ch-sp, (sc, ch 5, sc in 5th ch from hook, sc) in same sp, *[ch 1, (sc, ch 5, sc in 5th ch from hook, sc) in next ch sp] twice, (sc, ch 5, sc in 5th ch from hook, sc) in each of next 10 ch sps, [ch 1, (sc, ch 5, sc in 5th ch from hook, sc) in next ch sp] twice, (sc, ch 5, sc in 5th ch from hook, sc) in each of next 25 ch sps, [ch 1, (sc, ch 5, sc in 5th ch from hook, sc) in next ch sp] twice, (sc, ch 5, sc in 5th ch from hook, sc) in each of next 10 ch sps, *[ch 1, (sc, ch 5, sc in 5th ch from hook, sc) in next ch-sp] twice, (sc, ch 5, sc in 5th ch from hook, sc) in each of next 24 ch sps, join in beg sc.

Rnd 11: Sl st in next ch-5 sp, ch 1, sc in same sp, ch 3, dc in last sc made, (sc, ch 5, sc) in next ch-5 sp, [sc in next ch-5 sp, ch 3, dc in last sc made] 12 times, (sc, ch 5, sc) in next ch-5 sp, [sc in next ch-5 sp, ch 3, dc in last sc made] 27 times, (sc, ch 5, sc) in next ch-5 sp, [sc in next ch-5 sp, ch 3, dc in last sc made] 12 times, (sc, ch 5, sc) in next ch-5 sp, [sc in next ch-5 sp, ch 3, dc in last sc made] 26 times, join in first sc. Fasten off.

2nd & 3rd Motifs

Rnds 1–10: Rep row 1–rnd 10 of First Motif.

Rnd 11: Sl st in next ch-5 sp, ch 1, sc in same sp, ch 3, dc in last sc made, (sc, ch 5, sc) in next ch-5 sp, [sc in next ch-5 sp, ch 3, dc in last sc made] 12 times, sc in next ch-5 sp, ch 2, sl st in 2nd ch-5 sp made on previous motif, ch 2, sc in same ch-5 sp as last sc, (ch 1, sl st in next ch-3 sp on previous motif, ch 1, dc in last sc made, sc in next ch-5 sp on motif being joined] 26 times, ch 2, sl st in next ch-5 sp on motif, ch 2, sc in same ch-5 sp as last sc, [ch 3, dc in last sc made, sc in next ch-5 sp] 12 times, ch 5, sc in same ch-5 sp as last sc, [ch 3, dc in last sc made, sc in next ch-5 sp] 25 times, ch 3, dc in last sc made, join in beg sc. Fasten off.

4th Motif

Rnds 1–10: Rep row 1–rnd 10 of First Motif.

Rnd 11: Sl st in next ch-5 sp, ch 1, sc in same sp, ch 3, dc in last sc made, (sc, ch 5, sc) in next ch-5 sp, place marker in last ch-5 sp made, [sc in next ch-5 sp, ch 3, dc in last sc made] 12 times, sc in next ch-5 sp, ch 2, sl st in 2nd ch-5 sp made on previous motif, ch 2, sc in same ch-5 sp as last sc, [ch 1, sl st in next ch-3 sp on previous motif, ch 1, dc in last sc made, sc in next ch-5 sp on motif being joined] 26 times, ch 2, sl st in next ch-5 sp on previous motif, ch 2, sc in same ch-5 sp as last sc, [ch 3, dc in last sc made, sc in next ch-5 sp] 12 times, ch 5, sc in same ch-5 sp as last sc, [ch 3, dc in last sc made, sc in next ch-5 sp] 25 times, ch 3, dc in last sc made, join in beg sc. Fasten off.

2ND PANEL

Work same as First Panel through 3rd Motif.

4th Motif

Rnds 1–10: Rep row 1–rnd 10 of First Motif.

Rnd 11: Sl st in next ch-5 sp, ch 1, sc in same sp, ch 3, dc in last sc made, (sc, ch 5, sc) in next ch-5 sp, [sc in next ch-5 sp, ch 3, dc in last sc made] 12 times, sc in next ch-5 sp, ch 2, sl st in 2nd ch-5 sp made on previous motif, ch 2, sc in same ch-5 sp as last sc, [ch 1, sl st in next ch-3 sp on previous motif, ch 1, dc in last sc made, sc in next ch-5 sp on motif being joined] 26 times, ch 2, sl st in next ch-5 sp on previous motif, ch 2, sc in same ch-5 sp as last sc, [ch 3, dc in last sc made, sc in next ch-5 sp] 12 times, ch 5, sc in same ch-5 sp as last sc, place marker in last ch-5 sp made, [ch 3, dc in last sc made, sc in next ch-5 sp] 25 times, ch 3, dc in last sc made, join in beg sc. Fasten off.

Continued on page 27

Victorian Lace

Design by Melody MacDuffee

SKILL LEVEL

■■■□ INTERMEDIATE

FINISHED SIZE
43 x 58 inches

MATERIALS
- Medium (worsted) weight yarn:
  34 oz/1,700 yds/964g white
- Size I/9/5.5mm crochet hook or size
  needed to obtain gauge
- Tapestry needle

GAUGE
Rnds 1–5 = 4 inches in diameter

PATTERN NOTES
Weave in ends as work progresses.

Join rounds with a slip stitch unless
otherwise stated.

Chain-4 at beginning of treble crochet
rows counts as first treble crochet unless
otherwise stated.

SPECIAL STITCHES
Picot: Ch 4, sl st in 4th ch from hook.
2-picot loop (2-picot lp): [Ch 6, sl st in 4th
ch from hook] twice, ch 2.

INSTRUCTIONS

SQUARE
Make 20.
Rnd 1 (RS): Ch 6, *sl st* in first ch to form a

ring, ch 1, 12 sc in ring, join in beg sc. *(12 sc)*
Rnd 2: Ch 4, sk next st, *sl st in **back lp** (see
Stitch Guide) of next sc, ch 4, sk next sc,
rep from * around, join in joining sl st. *(6 sl
sts, 6 ch-4 sps)*
Rnd 3: Sl st in next ch-4 sp, ch 1, (sc, hdc,
3 dc, hdc, sc) in same sp *(petal)*, (sc, hdc,
3 dc, hdc, sc) in each of next 5 ch-4 sps *(5
petals)*, join in **front lp** (see Stitch Guide) of
beg sc, turn. *(6 petals)*
Rnd 4: Ch 5, sk first 6 sts, [sl st in front lp
of next sc, ch 5, sk next 6 sts] 5 times, join
in joining sl st, turn. *(6 sl sts, 6 ch-5 sps)*
Rnd 5: Sl st in next ch-5 sp, ch 1, (sc, hdc,
5 dc, hdc, sc) in same sp *(medium petal)*,
(sc, hdc, 5 dc, hdc, sc) in each of next 5
ch-5 sps *(5 medium petals)*, join in beg sc,
turn. *(6 medium petals)*
Rnd 6: Ch 6, sk first 8 sts, [sl st in front lp
of next sc, ch 6, sk next 8 sts] 5 times, join
in joining sl st, turn. *(6 sl sts, 6 ch-6 sps)*
Rnd 7: Sl st in next ch-6 sp, ch 1, (sc, hdc,
7 dc, hdc, sc) in same sp *(large petal)*, (sc,
hdc, 7 dc, hdc, sc) in each of next 5 ch-6
sps *(5 large petals)*, join in beg sc. Fasten
off. *(6 large petals)*
Rnd 8: Join yarn in first dc of any large
petal, **2-picot lp** (see Special Stitches), sk next
5 sts, sl st in next dc, 2-picot lp, sk next 4
sts, sl st in next dc, 2-picot lp, sk next 5 sts,
(sl st, 2-picot lp, sl st) in next st *(corner)*,
2-picot lp, sk next 4 sts, sl st in next dc,
2-picot lp, sk next 5 sts, sl st in next dc,
2-picot lp, sk next 4 sts, (sl st, 2-picot lp, sl
st) in next dc *(corner)*, 2-picot lp, sk next 5
sts, sl st in next dc, 2-picot lp, sk next 4 sts,

sl st in next dc, 2-picot lp, sk next 5 sts, (sl st 2-picot lp, sl st) in next dc *(corner)*, 2-picot lp, sk next 4 sts, sl st in next dc, 2-picot lp, sk next 5 sts, sl st in next dc, 2-picot lp, sk next 4 sts, sl st in same dc as joining sl st, 2-picot lp, join in joining sl st *(corner)*. Fasten off. *(16 2-picot lps)*

Rnd 9: Join yarn in any corner 2-picot lp, 2-picot lp, *sl st between picots of next 2-picot lp, 2-picot lp, rep from * to next corner 2-picot lp, corner in corner 2-picot lp, **sl st between picots of next 2-picot lp, 2-picot lp, rep from ** to next corner 2-picot lp, corner in corner 2-picot lp, ***sl st between picots of next 2-picot lp, 2-picot lp, rep from *** to next corner 2-picot lp, corner in corner 2-picot lp, ****sl st between picots of next 2-picot lp, 2-picot lp, rep from **** to joining sl st, sl st in same 2-picot lp as joining sl st, 2-picot lp, join in joining sl st. Fasten off. *(20 2-picot lps)*

Rnd 10: Rep rnd 9. *(24 2-picot lps at end of rnd)*

ASSEMBLY

Join Squares tog in 5 rows of 4 Squares each. Join Squares by working a joining rnd. Beg by working following rnd 11 on 1 Square:

Rnd 11: Rep rnd 9. *(28 2-picot lps at end of rnd)*

To join rem Squares, hold 2 Squares with WS tog and work rnd 11 with one-sided joining or two-sided joining as follows:

Rnd 11 (one-sided joining): Join yarn in any corner 2-picot lp, 2-picot lp, *sl st between picots of next 2-picot lp, 2-picot lp, rep from * to next corner 2-picot lp, corner in corner 2-picot lp, **sl st between picots of next 2-picot lp, 2-picot lp, rep from ** to next corner 2-picot lp, corner in corner 2-picot lp, ***sl st between picots of next 2-picot lp, 2-picot lp, rep from *** to next corner 2-picot lp, sl st in corner 2-picot lp, ch 2, picot, ch 4, sl st in picot of corresponding corner 2-picot lp on completed Square, ch 2, sl st in 3rd ch of ch-4, ch 2, sl st in same corner 2-picot lp on working Square, ****ch 2, picot, ch 1, sl st between picots of next corresponding 2-picot lp on completed Square, ch 1, picot, ch 2, sl st in next 2-picot lp on working Square, rep from **** across to next corner 2-picot lp, ch 4, sl st in picot of corresponding corner 2-picot lp on completed Square, ch 2, sl st in 3rd ch of ch-4, ch 2, picot, ch 2, join in beg sl st on working Square. Fasten off.

Rnd 11 (two-sided joining): Join yarn in any corner 2-picot lp, 2-picot lp, *sl st between picots of next 2-picot lp, 2-picot lp, rep from * to next corner 2-picot lp, corner in corner 2-picot lp, **sl st between picots of next 2-picot lp, 2-picot lp, rep from ** to next corner 2-picot lp, sl st in corner 2-picot lp, ch 2, picot, ch 4, sl st in picot of corresponding corner 2-picot lp on completed Square, ch 2, sl st in 3rd ch of ch-4, ch 2, sl st in same corner 2-picot lp on working Square, ***ch 2, picot, ch 1, sl st between picots of next corresponding 2-picot lp on completed Square, ch 1, picot, ch 2, sl st in next 2-picot lp on working Square, rep from *** across to next corner 2-picot lp, sl st in corner 2-picot lp, ch 2, picot, ch 4, sl st in picot of corresponding corner 2-picot lp on completed Square, ch 2, sl st in 3rd ch of ch-4, ch 2, sl st in same corner 2-picot lp on working Square, ****ch 2, picot, ch 1, sl st between picots of next corresponding 2-picot lp on completed Square, ch 1, picot, ch 2, sl st in next 2-picot lp on working Square, rep from **** across to next corner 2-picot lp, sl st in corner 2-picot lp, ch 4, sl st in picot of corresponding corner 2-picot lp on completed Square, ch 2, sl st in 3rd ch of ch-4, ch 2, picot, ch 2, join in beg sl st on working Square. Fasten off.

EDGING

Rnd 1: Hold piece with RS facing, join yarn in top right corner 2-picot lp, ch 9, sl st in same lp *(beg corner)*, *ch 9, sl st in next 2-picot lp, rep from * around, working (sl st, ch 9, sl st) in each rem corner 2-picot lp

(corner), join in joining sl st.
Rnd 2: Sl st in next ch-9 sp, ch 1, (sc, hdc, 9 dc, hdc, sc) in same sp, (sc, hdc, 3 hdc, hdc, sc) in each ch-9 sp around and (sc, hdc, 9 dc, hdc, sc) in each rem corner ch-9 sp, join in beg sc. Fasten off.■

PEARLS & LACE
Continued from page 8

Edging
Rnd 1 (RS): Ch 1, 3 sc in first dc, sc in each dc and 2 sc in each ch-2 sp across to last dc, 3 sc in last dc, working across next side in ends of rows, dc in end of row 75, *2 dc in end of next row, dc in end of next row, rep from * across, working across next side in unused lps of beg ch and in sps formed by sk chs, 3 sc in first lp, **work 2 sc in each ch-2 sp, sc in lp at base of each V-st, rep from ** across to last lp, 3 sc in last lp, working across next side in ends of rows, dc in end of row 1, ***2 dc in end of next row, dc in end of next row, rep from *** across to beg sc, **join** *(see Pattern Notes)* in beg sc. Fasten off. *(702 sc)*
Note: Cut approximately 10-inch length of sewing thread; tie 1 end onto new skein of buff; thread other end into sewing needle to thread pearls onto yarn. Thread pearls onto yarn.
Rnd 2: With WS facing and size H hook, join buff in any sc, ch 1, bead sc *(see Special Stitches)* in same sc, *ch 5, sk next 2 sc, bead sc in next sc, rep from * around, join in beg bead sc.
Rnd 3: Sc in next ch-5 sp, *ch 5, sc in next ch-5 sp, rep from * around, join in beg sc.
Rnd 4: Bead sc in next ch-5 sp, *ch 5, bead sc in next sc, rep from * around, join in beg bead sc.

Rnd 5: Sc in next ch-5 sp, *ch 5, sc in next ch-5 sp, rep from * around, join in beg sc. Fasten off.

FLOWER
Make 8.
Rnd 1 (RS): With size J hook and soft white and leaving a 10-inch end, ch 5, join with sl st in first ch to form a ring, ch 1, [sc in ring, ch 5] 34 times, join in first sc. Fasten off, leaving a 10-inch end.

ASSEMBLY
With tapestry needle, weave first 10-inch end in ring and pull tight to close bottom of Flower. Leave end for attaching to afghan. Weave rem end in top of ring and pull tight to close Flower. Secure end.

LEAF
Make 16.
With size J hook and old sage, ch 6, sc in 2nd ch from hook, hdc in each of next 2 chs, dc in next ch, 7 dc in last ch, working in unused lps on opposite side of beg ch, dc in next ch, hdc in each of next 2 chs, sc in last ch, join in first sc. Fasten off, leaving 10-inch end.

FINISHING
Sew 2 Leaves to back of each Flower. Sew 2 Flowers to each corner of afghan. ■

LIME LACE
Continued from page 14

beg ch-6, turn. *(86 dc, 17 sc, 34 ch-3 sps)*
Rows 6–105: [Rep rows 2–5 consecutively] 25 times.
Rows 106 & 107: Rep rows 2 and 3.

EDGING
Rnd 1 (RS): Ch 3, work 169 dc evenly spaced across to last st, 5 dc in last st *(corner)*, working

across next side in ends of rows, work 201 dc evenly spaced across side, working across next side in unused lps of beg ch, 5 dc in first lp *(corner)*, work 169 dc evenly spaced across to last lp, 5 dc in last lp *(corner)*, working across next side in ends of rows, work 201 dc evenly spaced across side to beg ch-3, 4 dc in same st as beg ch-3 *(corner)*, **join** *(see Pattern Notes)* in 3rd ch of beg ch-3, turn. *(760 dc)*

Rnd 2: Ch 4 *(see Pattern Notes)*, *sk next dc, dc in next dc, ch 1, rep from * around, join in 3rd ch of beg ch-4, turn. *(380 dc)*

Rnd 3: Ch 1, sc in first dc, ch 5, sk next dc, *sc in next dc, ch 5, sk next dc, rep from * around, ch 2, join with dc in beg sc, turn.

Rnd 4: Ch 1, sc in sp formed by joining dc, *ch 5, sc in next ch-5 sp, rep from * around, ch 2, join with dc in beg sc, turn.

Rnd 5: Ch 1, sc in sp formed by joining dc, *ch 3, [tr, ch 3, sl st in first ch, ch 1] 3 times in next ch-5 sp, ch 2 **, sc in next ch-5 sp, rep from * around, ending last rep at **, join in beg sc. Fasten off. ∎

TREE BLOSSOMS
Continued from page 17

ch 5, sk next 3 ch-3 sps, sc in next ch-3 sp, ch 6, sk next 3 ch-3 sps, sk next ch of beg ch-6, dtr in next ch of same ch-6, ch 7, sc in 2nd ch from hook, sc in each of next 5 chs, turn, sl st in first ch of next ch-6 sp, turn, sc in each of next 6 sc, ch 2, hdc in end of ch-7, turn. *(9 tree trunks)*

Row 5: Ch 5 *(see Pattern Notes)*, [tr, ch 1] 4 times in next ch-2 sp, sk next 2 sc, tr in next sc, *ch 3, sk next ch-6 sp, sc in next sc, ch 3, sk next ch-5 sp, sk next 3 sc, tr in next sc, ch 1, [tr, ch 1] 9 times in next ch-5 sp, sk next 2 sc, tr in next sc, rep from * 8 times, ch 3, sk next ch-6 sp, sc in next sc, ch 3, sk next ch-5 sp, sk next 3 sc, tr in next sc, ch 1, [tr, ch 1] 4 times in sp formed by beg 4 sk chs of beg ch-15 of previous row, tr in same sp, turn.

Row 6: Ch 3, [sc in next ch-1 sp, ch 3] 4 times, *sk next 4 ch sps, [sc in next ch-1 sp, ch 3] 8 times, rep from * 8 times, sk next 4 ch sps, [sc in next ch-1 sp, ch 3] 3 times, sc in next ch-1 sp, ch 1, hdc in 4th ch of beg ch-5, turn.

Row 7: Ch 1, sc in first hdc, *ch 6, sk next 3 ch-3 sp, dtr in next ch-3 sp, ch 7, sc in 2nd ch from hook, sc in each of next 5 chs, turn, sl st in first ch of next ch-6 sp, turn, sc in each of next 6 sc, ch 5, working in unused lps on opposite side of ch-7, sc in each of next 6 chs *(tree trunk)*, ch 5, sk next 3 ch-3 sps **, sc in next ch-3 sp, rep from * 9 times, ending last rep at **, sc in sp formed by beg ch-3, turn. *(10 tree trunks)*

Row 8: Ch 1, sc in first sc, *ch 3, sk next 5 chs, sk next 3 sc, tr in next sc, ch 1, [tr, ch 1] 9 times in next ch-5 sp, sk next 2 sc, tr in next sc, ch 3, sk next 5 chs, sc in next sc, rep from * 9 times, turn.

Row 9: Ch 6, sk next 2 ch sps, * [sc in next ch-1 sp, ch 3] 8 times, sk next 4 ch sps, rep from * 8 times, [sc in next ch-1 sp, ch 3] 7 times, sc in next ch-1 sp, ch 1, sk next ch-1 sp, dtr in last sc, turn.

Rows 10–45: [Rep rows 4–9 consecutively] 6 times. At end of last row, **do not turn.**

Edging
Row 1: Ch 1, working across next side, sc evenly spaced across to row 1, ch 9, working across next side, sk next 5 chs, sc in unused lp of next ch, ch 5, sk unused lp of next ch, sc in unused lp of next ch, *ch 5, sk next 5 chs, sc in unused lp of next ch, ch 5, sk unused lp of next ch, sc in unused lp of next ch, ch 5, sk next 5 chs, sc in unused lp of next ch, rep from * 8 times, leaving rem side unworked, turn.

Row 2: Ch 3, *[tr, ch 1] 8 times in next ch-5 sp, tr in same sp, ch 3, sc in sc in row below, ch 3, rep from * across, ending with sc in 3rd ch of ch-9, turn.

Row 3: *Ch 3, sc in ch-3 sp, [ch 3, sc in next ch-3 sp] 7 times, rep from * across, ending with ch 5, sc in end st in row below, working across next side, sc evenly spaced across to beg sc of row 45. Fasten off. ∎

SERENE MEADOW
Continued from page 21

ASSEMBLY
Join aran with sc in marked ch-5 sp on First Panel, ch 2, sc in marked ch-5 sp on 2nd Panel, *[ch 2, sc in next ch-3 sp on First Panel, ch 2, sc in next ch-3 sp on 2nd Panel] 12 times, ch 2, sc in next joining sl st on First Panel, ch 2, sc in next joining sl st on 2nd Panel, rep from * twice, [ch 2, sc in next ch-3 sp on First Panel, ch 2, sc in next ch-3 sp on Panel 2] 12 times, ch 2, sc in next ch-5 sp on First Panel, ch 2, sc in next ch-5 sp on 2nd Panel. Fasten off.

EDGING
Rnd 1: Join aran in first ch-5 sp made on last rnd of 4th Motif on 2nd Panel, (beg V-st, ch 2, V-st) in same sp *(beg corner)*, *[V-st in each of next 12 ch-3 sps, V-st in sl st of motif joining] 3 times, V-st in each of next 12 ch-3 sps, (V-st, ch 2, V-st) in next ch-5 sp *(corner)*, V-st in each of next 27 ch-3 sps, V-st in panel joining, V-st in each of next 27 ch-3 sps **, (V-st, ch 2, V-st) in next ch-5 sp *(corner)*, rep from * once ending rep at **, join in 3rd ch of beg ch-4.

Rnd 2: Sl st in first ch-sp, ch 1, sc in same sp, ch 3, (sc, ch 3, sc) in next ch-2 sp *(corner)*, ch-3, *sc in next V-st, ch 3, rep from * across to next corner ch-2 sp, (sc, ch 3, sc) in corner ch-2 sp *(corner)*, **sc in next V-st, ch 3, rep from ** across to next corner ch-2 sp, (sc, ch 3, sc) in corner ch-2 sp *(corner)*, ***sc in next V-st, ch 3, rep from *** across to next corner ch-2 sp, (sc, ch 3, sc) in corner ch-2 sp *(corner)*, ****sc in next V-st, ch 3, rep from **** across to beg

sc, join in beg sc. Fasten off.

Rnd 3: Join light green in 2nd ch-3 sp made on previous rnd, (beg V-st, ch 2, V-st) in same sp *(beg corner)*, *V-st in each of next 54 ch-3 sps, (V-st, ch 2, V-st) in next corner ch-3 sp *(corner)*, V-st in each of next 59 ch-3 sps **,(V-st, ch 2, V-st) in next ch-3 sp *(corner)*, rep from * once, ending rep at **, join in 3rd ch of beg ch-4. Fasten off.

Rnd 4: Join medium green with sc in first corner ch-2 sp on previous rnd, ch 3, sc in same sp *(beg corner)*, ch 3, *sc in next ch-1 sp, ch 3, rep from * across to next corner ch-2 sp, (sc, ch 3, sc) in corner ch-2 sp *(corner)*, ch 3, **sc in next ch-1 sp, ch 3, rep from ** across to next corner ch-2 sp, (sc, ch 3, sc) in corner ch-2 sp *(corner)*, ch 3, ***sc in next ch-1 sp, ch 3, rep from *** across to next corner ch-2 sp, (sc, ch 3, sc) in corner ch-2 sp *(corner)*, ch 3, ****sc in next ch-1 sp, ch 3, rep from * across to beg sc, join in beg sc. Fasten off.

Rnd 5: Join dark green with sc in first corner ch-3 sp made on previous rnd, ch 3, dc in last sc made, sc in same sp, [ch 3, dc in last sc made, sc in next ch-3 sp] 58 times, ch 3, dc in last sc made, sc in same sp, [ch 3, dc in last sc made, sc in next ch-3 sp] 63 times, ch 3, dc in last sc made, sc in same sp, [ch 3, dc in last sc made, sc in next ch-3 sp] 58 times, ch 3, dc in last sc made, sc in same sp, [ch 3, dc in last sc made, sc in next ch-3 sp] 62 times, ch 3, dc in last sc made, join in beg sc. Fasten off. ∎

Antique Edgings

Turn an ordinary afghan into something special by adding a beautiful edging. These lovely afghans will be cherished items to hand down to the next generation.

Aran Afghan

Design by Lucille LaFlamme

SKILL LEVEL
■■■□ INTERMEDIATE

FINISHED SIZE
35 x 53 inches

MATERIALS
- Red Heart Super Saver medium (worsted) weight yarn (7 oz/ 364 yds/198g per skein): 3 skeins #313 aran
- Size H/8/5mm crochet hook or size needed to obtain gauge
- Tapestry needle

GAUGE
Rnds 1–3 = 3½ inches

PATTERN NOTES
Weave in ends as work progresses.

Join rounds with a slip stitch unless otherwise stated.

Chain-3 at beginning of double crochet rows counts as first double crochet unless otherwise stated.

SPECIAL STITCHES
Beginning cluster (beg cl): Ch 3, keeping back last lp of each dc on hook, 2 dc in indicated st, yo and draw through all 3 lps on hook.
Cluster (cl): Keeping back last lp of each dc on hook, 3 dc in indicated st, yo and draw through all 4 lps on hook.
Picot: Ch 4, sl st in last st made.

INSTRUCTIONS

MOTIF
Make 54.
Rnd 1: Ch 5, join with sl st in first ch to form a ring, **ch 3** *(see Pattern Notes)*, dc in ring, ch 2, [2 dc in ring, ch 2] 7 times, join in 3rd ch of beg ch-3. *(16 dc, 8 ch-2 sps)*
Rnd 2: Sl st in next dc, sl st in next ch-2 sp, **beg cl** *(see Special Stitches)* in same sp, ch 4, sc in next ch-2 sp, ch 4, *cl *(see Special Stitches)* in next ch-2 sp, ch 4, sc in next ch-2 sp, ch 4, rep from * around, join in top of beg cl. *(4 cl, 4 sc, 8 ch-2 sps)*
Rnd 3: Ch 3, (dc, ch 3, 2 dc) in same st *(beg corner)*, ch 3, *cl in next sc, ch 3, (2 dc, ch 3, 2 dc) in next cl *(corner)*, ch 3, rep from * around, join in 3rd ch of beg ch-3. *(4 cl, 16 dc, 12 ch-3 sps)*
Rnd 4: Ch 3, dc in next dc, *(dc, ch 5, dc) in next ch-3 sp *(corner)*, dc in each of next 2 dc, ch 2, [dc, ch 1] twice in next cl, dc in same cl, ch 2, dc in each of next 2 dc, rep from * twice, (dc, ch 5, dc) in next ch-3 sp *(corner)*, dc in each of next 2 dc, ch 2, [dc, ch 1] twice in next cl, dc in same cl, ch 2, join in 3rd ch of beg ch-3. *(36 dc, 4 ch-5 sps, 8 ch-2 sps, 8 ch-1 sps)*
Rnd 5: Ch 3, dc in each of next 2 dc, *7 dc in next ch-5 sp *(corner)*, dc in each of next 3 dc, 2 dc in next sp, [dc in next dc, dc in next sp] twice, dc in next dc, 2 dc in next sp, dc in each of next 3 dc, rep from * twice, 7 dc in next ch-5 sp *(corner)*, dc in

Continued on page 44

Frosty Lace

Design by Laura Gebhardt

SKILL LEVEL

■■■□ INTERMEDIATE

FINISHED SIZE
48 x 57 inches

MATERIALS
- Red Heart Super Saver medium (worsted) weight yarn (7 oz/ 364 yds/198g per skein):
    5 skeins #661 frosty green
- Size H/8/5mm crochet hook or size needed to obtain gauge
- Tapestry needle
- Stitch markers

GAUGE
10 dc = 3 inches

PATTERN NOTES
Weave in ends as work progresses.

Join rounds with a slip stitch unless otherwise stated.

Chain-3 at beginning of double crochet rows counts as first double crochet unless otherwise stated.

Chain-3 at beginning of half double crochet rows counts as first half double crochet and chain-1 space unless otherwise stated.

Chain-4 at beginning of treble crochet rows counts as first treble crochet and chain-1 space unless otherwise stated.

Chain-5 at beginning of double crochet rows counts as first double crochet and chain-2 space unless otherwise stated.

SPECIAL STITCHES
V-stitch (V-st): (Dc, ch 1, dc) in indicated st or sp.
Beginning large V-stitch (beg large V-st): Ch 5, dc in indicated st or sp.
Large V-stitch (large V-st): (Dc, ch 2, dc) in indicated st or sp.
Beginning shell (beg shell): Ch 3, (dc, ch 2, 2 dc) in indicated st or sp.
Shell: (2 dc, ch 2, 2 dc) in indicated st or sp.
Beginning picot shell (beg picot shell): Ch 3, (dc, ch 4, sl st in 3rd ch from hook, ch 1, 2 dc) in indicated st or sp.
Picot shell: (2 dc, ch 4, sl st in 3rd ch from hook, ch 1, 2 dc) in indicated st or sp.

INSTRUCTIONS

CENTER
Row 1: Ch 167, dc in 4th ch from hook *(beg 3 sk chs count as a dc)*, dc in each ch across, turn. *(165 dc)*
Row 2: Ch 1, sc in first dc, *ch 5, sk next 3 dc, sc in next dc, rep from * across to last 4 sts, ch 5, sk next 3 dc, sc in 3rd ch of beg 3 sk chs, turn. *(42 sc, 4 ch-5 sps)*
Row 3: Ch 4 *(see Pattern Notes)*, V-st *(see Special Stitches)* in next ch-5 sp, *ch 1, V-st in next ch-5 sp, rep from * across to last sc, ch 1, tr in last sc, turn. *(41 V-sts, 2 tr)*

Continued on page 45

French Stripes

Design by Christine L. Walter

SKILL LEVEL
 ■■■□ INTERMEDIATE

FINISHED SIZE
52 x 76 inches

MATERIALS
- Lion Brand Vanna's Choice medium (worsted) weight yarn (3½ oz/170 yds/100g per skein):
    7 skeins #108 dusty blue
    5 skeins each #105 silver blue and #170 pea green
- Size I/9/5.5mm crochet hook or size needed to obtain gauge
- Tapestry needle

GAUGE
16 sts = 4 inches; 6 rows = 4 inches

PATTERN NOTES
Weave in ends as work progresses.

Chain-3 at beginning of double crochet rows counts as first double crochet unless otherwise stated.

Chain-5 at beginning of double crochet rows counts as first double crochet and chain-2 space unless otherwise stated.

SPECIAL STITCH
Shell: (Sc, ch 3, 4 dc) in indicated st.
Cluster (cl): Holding back last lp of each dc on hook, 3 dc in indicated st, yo and draw through all 4 lps on hook.

Triple picot: [Ch 3, sl st in first ch] 3 times, sl st in indicated st.

INSTRUCTIONS

CENTER
Row 1 (RS): With silver blue, ch 190, **shell** *(see Special Stitches)* in 2nd ch from hook, *sk next 3 chs, shell in next ch, rep from * to last 4 chs, sk next 3 chs, sc in last ch, **change color** *(see Stitch Guide)* to dusty blue in last sc, turn. *(47 shells, 1 sc)*
Row 2: Ch 3 *(see Pattern Notes)*, *sk next dc, **dc dec** *(see Stitch Guide)* in next 2 sts, ch 3, sk next dc, sc in next ch, rep from * across, change color to pea green in last sc, turn. *(48 dc, 17 sc)*
Row 3: Ch 1, shell in first sc, *sk next 3 chs, sk next st, shell in next sc, rep from * across, sk next 3 chs, sk next st, sc in 3rd ch of beg ch-3, change color to silver blue in last sc, turn. *(47 shells, 1 sc)*
Row 4: Rep row 2, changing to dusty blue in last sc.
Row 5: Rep row 3, changing to pea green in last sc.
Row 6: Rep row 2, changing to silver blue in last sc.
Row 7: Rep row 3, changing to dusty blue in last sc.
Rows 8–73: [Rep rows 2–7 consecutively] 11 times.
Rows 74–78: Rep rows 2–8. At end of row 78, fasten off.

Continued on page 46

Lacy Cross-Stitch

Design by Anne Halliday

SKILL LEVEL

 INTERMEDIATE

FINISHED SIZE

54 x 68 inches, excluding fringe

MATERIALS

- Red Heart Soft Yarn medium (worsted) weight yarn (5 oz/ 256 yds/140g per skein): 12 skeins #9520 seafoam
- Size H/8/5mm crochet hook or size needed to obtain gauge
- Tapestry needle

GAUGE

16 sts = 4 inches

PATTERN NOTES

Weave in ends as work progresses.

Join rounds with a slip stitch unless otherwise stated.

Chain-4 at beginning of double crochet rows counts as first double crochet and chain-1 space unless otherwise stated.

INSTRUCTIONS

CENTER

Row 1 (WS): Ch 272, sc in 2nd ch from hook, *ch 1, sk next ch, sc in next ch, rep from * across, turn. *(271 sts)*

Row 2 (RS): Ch 4 *(see Pattern Notes)*, sk next sc, tr in next sc, ch 1, working in front of tr just made, tr in 2nd sk sc, ch 1, *sk next sc, tr in next sc, ch 1, working in front of tr just made, tr in sk sc, ch 1, rep from * across to last sc, dc in last sc, turn. *(134 tr, 2 dc)*

Row 3: Ch 1, sc in first dc, *ch 1, sk next ch-1 sp, sc in next dc, rep from * to beg ch-4, ch 1, sc in 3rd ch of beg ch-4, turn. *(271 sts)*

Row 4: Ch 4, sk next sc, tr in next sc, ch 1, working behind tr just made, tr in 2nd sk sc, ch 1, *sk next sc, tr in next sc, ch 1, working behind tr just made, tr in sk sc, ch 1, rep from * across to last sc, dc in last sc, turn. *(134 tr, 2 dc)*

Row 5: Ch 1, sc in first dc, *ch 1, sk next ch-1 sp, sc in next dc, rep from * to beg ch-4, ch 1, sc in 3rd ch of beg ch-4, turn.

Rows 6–105: [Rep rows 2–5 consecutively] 25 times.

EDGING

Rnd 1: Ch 1, sc in first sc, *ch 1, sc in next sc, rep from * across, ch 2 *(corner)*, working across next side in ends of rows, sc in first sc row, **ch 3, sk next dc row, sc in next sc row, rep from ** across, ch 2 *(corner)*, working across next side in unused lps of beg ch, sc in first lp, ***ch 1, sk next lp, sc in next lp, rep from *** across, ch 2 *(corner)*, working across next side in ends of rows, sc in first sc row, ****ch 3, sk next dc row, sc in next sc row, rep from **** across to beg sc, ch 2 *(corner)*, **join** *(see Pattern Notes)* in beg sc.

Continued on page 46

Lacy Squares With Scallop Edging

Design by Anne Halliday

SKILL LEVEL

 ■■■□ INTERMEDIATE

FINISHED SIZE
46 x 65 inches

MATERIALS

- Red Heart Super Saver medium (worsted) weight yarn (7 oz/ 364 yds/198g per skein): 7 skeins #327 light coral
- Size H/8/5mm crochet hook or size needed to obtain gauge
- Tapestry needle

GAUGE
Square = 4½ inches

PATTERN NOTES
Weave in ends as work progresses.

Join rounds with a slip stitch unless otherwise stated.

Chain-3 at beginning of double crochet rows counts as first double crochet unless otherwise stated.

Chain-4 at beginning of double crochet rows counts as first double crochet and chain-1 space unless otherwise stated.

Chain-5 at beginning of double crochet rows counts as first double crochet and chain-2 space unless otherwise stated.

SPECIAL STITCHES
Beginning cluster (beg cl): Holding back last lp of each dc on hook, dc in 3 indicated sts, yo and draw through all 4 lps on hook.
Cluster (cl): Holding back last lp of each dc on hook, dc in 4 indicated sts, yo and draw through all 4 lps on hook.
Picot cluster (picot cl): Ch 4, holding back last lp of each dc on hook, 2 dc in 3rd ch from hook, yo and draw through all 3 lps on hook.

INSTRUCTIONS

SQUARE
Make 117.
Rnd 1 (RS): Ch 2, 8 sc in 2nd ch from hook, **join** *(see Pattern Notes)* in beg sc. *(8 sc)*
Rnd 2: Ch 3 *(see Pattern Notes)*, dc in same sc, 2 dc in next sc, ch 3, [2 dc in each of next 2 sc, ch 3] 3 times, join in 3rd ch of beg ch-3. *(16 dc, 4 ch-3 sps)*
Rnd 3: Ch 2, **beg cl** *(see Special Stitches)* in next 3 dc, ch 2, (dc, ch 5, dc) in next ch-3 sp *(corner)*, ch 2, *cl *(see Special Stitches)* in next 4 dc, ch 2, (dc, ch 5, dc) in next ch-3 sp *(corner)*, ch 2, rep from * twice, join in top of beg cl. *(4 cl, 8 dc, 4 ch-5 sps, 8 ch-2 sps)*
Rnd 4: Ch 3, 2 dc in next ch-2 sp, dc in next dc, (3 dc, ch 3, 3 dc) in next ch-5 sp *(corner)*, dc in next dc, *[2 dc in next ch-2 sp, dc in next st] twice, (3 dc, ch 3, 3 dc) in next ch-5 sp *(corner)*, dc in next dc, rep from * twice, 2 dc in next ch-2 sp, join in 3rd ch of beg ch-3. Fasten off. *(52 dc, 4 ch-3 sps)*

ASSEMBLY

Working in **back lps** (*see Stitch Guide*) only, sew Squares together with RS facing, carefully matching stitches. Sew Squares together in 13 rows of 9 Squares each.

EDGING

Rnd 1 (RS): Hold afghan with RS facing and 1 short end at top, join yarn with sc in 12th dc to right of corner ch-3 sp in upper right-hand corner, sc in each of next 11 dc, (sc, ch 3, sc) in next ch-3 sp *(corner)*, sc in each of next 13 dc, *hdc in next ch sp, ch 1, hdc in next ch sp, sc in each of next 13 dc, rep from * 7 times, (sc, ch 3, sc) in next corner ch-3 sp *(corner)*, sc in each of next 13 dc, **hdc in next ch sp, ch 1, hdc in next ch sp, sc in each of next 13 dc, rep from ** 11 times, (sc, ch 3, sc) in next corner ch-3 sp *(corner)*, sc in each of next 13 dc, ***hdc

in next ch sp, ch 1, hdc in next ch sp, sc in each of next 13 dc, rep from *** 7 times, (sc, ch 3, sc) in next corner ch-3 sp *(corner)*, sc in each of next 13 dc, ****hdc in next ch sp, ch 1, hdc in next ch sp, sc in each of next 13 dc, rep from **** 10 times, hdc in next ch sp, ch 1, hdc in next ch sp, sc in next sc, join in beg sc.

Rnd 2: Ch 1, sc in same sc, sc in each of next 10 sc, ch 1, sk next 2 sc, (dc, ch 1, dc, ch 3, dc, ch 1, dc) in next ch-3 sp *(corner)*, *ch 1, sk next 2 sc, sc in each of next 11 sc, ch 1, sk next 2 sc, (dc, ch 3, dc) in next ch-1 sp, rep from * 6 times, ch 1, sk next 2 sc, sc in each of next 11 sc, ch 1, (dc, ch 1, dc, ch 3, dc, ch 1, dc) in next ch-3 sp *(corner)*, **ch 1, sk next 2 sc, sc in each of next 11 sc, ch 1, sk next 2 sc, (dc, ch 3, dc) in next ch-1 sp, rep from ** 10 times, ch 1, sk next 2 sc, sc in each of next 11 sc, ch 1, (dc, ch 1, dc, ch 3, dc, ch 1, dc) in next ch-3 sp *(corner)*, ***ch 1, sk next 2 sc, sc in each of next 11 sc, ch 1, sk next 2 sc, (dc, ch 3, dc) in next ch-1 sp, rep from *** 6 times, ch 1, sk next 2 sc, sc in each of next 11 sc, ch 1, (dc, ch 1, dc, ch 3, dc, ch 1, dc) in next ch-3 sp *(corner)*, ****ch 1, sk next 2 sc, sc in each of next 11 sc, ch 1, sk next 2 sc, (dc, ch 3, dc) in next ch-1 sp, rep from **** 6 times, rep from **** to beg sc, join in beg sc.

Rnd 3: Ch 1, sk first sc, sc in each of next 9 sc, ch 1, sk next sc, sk next ch-1 sp, *dc in next dc, ch 1, dc in next ch-1 sp, ch 1, dc in next dc, ch 1, [dc, ch 1] 3 times in next ch-3 sp, dc in next dc, ch 1, dc in next ch-1 sp, ch 1, dc in next dc, ch 1, sk next ch, sk next sc, sc in each of next 9 sc, ch 1, sk next sc, sk next ch, **dc in next dc, ch 1, [dc, ch 1] 3 times in next ch-3 sp, dc in next dc, ch 1, sk next ch, sk next sc, sc in each of next 9 sc, ch 1, sk next sc, sk next ch, rep from ** across to first dc of next corner, rep from * twice, dc in next dc, ch 1, dc in next ch-1 sp, ch 1, dc in next dc, ch 1, [dc, ch 1] 3 times in next ch-3 sp, dc in next dc, ch 1, dc in next ch-1 sp, ch 1, dc in next dc, ch 1,

Continued on page 47

Vintage Florals

Design by Lucille LaFlamme

SKILL LEVEL
 INTERMEDIATE

FINISHED SIZE
48 x 65 inches

MATERIALS
• Red Heart Super Saver medium (worsted) weight yarn (7 oz/ 364 yds/198g per skein):
    3 skeins #311 white
    2 skeins each #372 rose pink and #376 burgundy
    1 skein #322 pale yellow
• Red Heart Soft Yarn medium (worsted) weight yarn (5 oz/256 yds/140g per skein):
    3 skeins #9522 leaf
• Size G/6/4mm crochet hook or size needed to obtain gauge
• Tapestry needle

GAUGE
Rnds 1–3 = 3½ inches in diameter

PATTERN NOTES
Weave in ends as work progresses.

Join rounds with a slip stitch unless otherwise stated.

Chain-3 at beginning of double crochet rounds counts as first double crochet unless otherwise stated.

Chain-6 at beginning of double crochet rounds counts as first double crochet and chain-3 space unless otherwise stated.

SPECIAL STITCHES

Beginning cluster (beg cl): Ch 3, holding back last lp of each dc on hook, 2 dc in indicated st, yo and draw through all 3 lps on hook.

Cluster (cl): Holding back last lp of each dc on hook, 3 dc in indicated st, yo and draw through all 4 lps on hook.

Picot: Ch 3, sl st in last st made.

INSTRUCTIONS

MOTIF

Make 48.

Rnd 1 (RS): With pale yellow, ch 5, sl st in first ch to form ring, ch 1, 16 sc in ring, join in beg sc. Fasten off. *(16 sc)*

Rnd 2: Join burgundy in any sc, **ch 6** *(see Pattern Notes)*, sk next sc, *dc in next sc, ch 3, sk next sc, rep from * 6 times, join in 3rd ch of beg ch-6. *(8 dc, 8 ch-3 sps)*

Rnd 3: *(Sc, hdc, 3 dc, hdc, sc) in next ch-3 sp *(petal)*, rep from * 7 times, join in beg sc. Fasten off. *(8 petals)* Turn.

Rnd 4: Join rose pink with sc around back strand of last sc of any petal, *ch 5, sc around back strand of last sc on next petal, rep from * around, join in beg sc, turn. *(8 sc, 8 ch-5 sps)*

Rnd 5: *(Sc, hdc, 6 dc, hdc, sc) in next ch-5 sp *(medium petal)*, rep from * 7 times, join in beg sc. Fasten off. *(8 medium petals)*

Rnd 6: Join leaf with sc in 6th dc of any medium petal, *ch 5 *(corner)*, sc in first dc of next medium petal, ch 4, sk next 4 dc, sc in next dc, ch 4, sc in first dc of next medium petal, ch 4, sk next 4 dc **, sc in next dc, rep from * 3 times, ending last rep at **, join in beg sc. *(16 sc, 12 ch-4 sps, 4 ch-5 sps)*

Rnd 7: Sl st in next ch-5 sp, **ch 3** *(see Pattern Notes)*, (3 dc, ch 3, 4 dc) in same sp *(beg corner)*, *ch 3, sc in next ch-4 sp, [ch 4, sc in next ch-4 sp] twice, ch 3 **, (4 dc, ch 3, 4 dc) in next corner ch-5 sp *(corner)*, rep from * 3 times, ending last rep at **, join in 3rd ch of beg ch-3. Fasten off. *(32 dc, 12 sc, 8 ch-4 sps, 16 ch-3 sps)*

Rnd 8: Join white in first dc of any corner, ch 3, dc in each of next 3 dc, *5 dc in next corner ch-3 sp *(corner)*, dc in each of next 4 dc, 3 dc in next ch-3 sp, dc in next sc, [4 dc in next ch-4 sp, dc in next sc] twice, dc in next dc, 3 dc in next ch-3 sp **, dc in each of next 4 dc, rep from * 3 times, ending last rep at **, join in 3rd ch of beg ch-3. Fasten off. *(120 dc)*

ASSEMBLY

With tapestry needle and white and working in **back lps** *(see Stitch Guide)* only, sew Motifs together with RS facing, carefully matching stitches. Sew Motifs together in 8 rows of 6 Motifs each.

EDGING

Rnd 1: Hold piece with RS facing and 1 short end at top, join white with sc in 3rd dc in right-hand corner, ch 3, sc in same dc *(corner)*, *[ch 5, sk next 4 dc, sc in next dc] 5 times, ch 5, sc in joining st of Motifs, rep from * 4 times, [ch 5, sk next 4 dc, sc in next dc] 5 times, sk next 4 dc, (sc, ch 3, sc) in next dc *(corner)*, **[ch 5, sk next 4 dc, sc in next dc] 5 times, ch 5, sc in joining st of Motifs, rep from ** 6 times, [ch 5, sk next 4 dc, sc in next dc] 5 times, sk next 4 dc, (sc, ch 3, sc) in next dc *(corner)*, ***[ch 5, sk next 4 dc, sc in next dc] 5 times, ch 5, sc in joining st of Motifs, rep from *** 4 times, [ch 5, sk next 4 dc, sc in next dc] 5 times, sk next 4 dc, (sc, ch 3, sc) in next dc *(corner)*, ****[ch 5, sk next 4 dc, sc in next dc] 5 times, ch 5, sc in joining st of Motifs, rep from **** 6 times, [ch 5, sk next 4 dc, sc in next dc] 5 times, sk next 4 dc, join in beg sc.

Rnd 2: *(2 sc, ch 3, 2 sc) in next ch-3 sp *(corner)*, (3 sc, ch 3, 3 sc) in each ch-5 sp to next corner ch-3 sp, rep from * around, join in beg sc. Fasten off.

Rnd 3: Join burgundy with sc in any corner ch-3 sp, (hdc, 3 dc, hdc, sc) in same sp

(beg corner), ch 1, *(sc, hdc, 3 dc, hdc, sc) in next ch-3 sp, ch 1, rep from * across to next corner ch-3 sp, (sc, hdc, 3 dc, hdc, 3 sc) in corner ch-3 sp *(corner)*, **(sc, hdc, 3 dc, hdc, sc) in next ch-3 sp, ch 1, rep from ** across to next corner ch-3 sp, (sc, hdc, 3 dc, hdc, 3 sc) in corner ch-3 sp *(corner)*, ***(sc, hdc, 3 dc, hdc, sc) in next ch-3 sp, ch 1, rep from *** across to next corner ch-3 sp, (sc, hdc, 3 dc, hdc, 3 sc) in corner ch-3 sp *(corner)*, ****(sc, hdc, 3 dc, hdc, sc) in next ch-3 sp, ch 1, rep from **** across to beg sc, join in beg sc. Fasten off.

Rnd 4: Join white with sc in 2nd dc of 3-dc group of any corner, ch 4, sc in same dc *(beg corner)*, *ch 4, (sc, ch 3, sc) in 2nd dc of next petal, rep from * across to next 2nd dc of next corner, (sc, ch 4, sc) in corner dc *(corner)*, **ch 4, (sc, ch 3, sc) in 2nd dc of next petal, rep from ** across to next 2nd dc of next corner, (sc, ch 4, sc) in corner dc *(corner)*, ***ch 4, (sc, ch 3, sc) in 2nd dc of next petal, rep from *** across to next 2nd dc of next corner, (sc, ch 4, sc) in corner dc *(corner)*, ****ch 4, (sc, ch 3, sc) in 2nd dc of next petal, rep from **** across to beg sc, join in beg sc.

Rnd 5: Ch 3, dc in next ch-4 sp, **picot** *(see Special Stitches)*, [2 dc in same sp, picot] twice, dc in same sp *(beg corner)*, ch 3, sc in next ch-4 sp, *ch 2, (dc, picot, dc) in next ch-3 sp, ch 2, sc in next sp, rep from * across to next corner ch-3 sp, ch 3, (dc, picot, 2 dc, picot, 2 dc, picot, dc) in corner ch-3 sp *(corner)*, **ch 2, (dc, picot, dc) in next ch-3 sp, ch 2, sc in next sp, rep from ** across to next corner ch-3 sp, ch 3, (dc, picot, 2 dc, picot, 2 dc, picot, dc) in corner ch-3 sp *(corner)*, ***ch 2, (dc, picot, dc) in next ch-3 sp, ch 2, sc in next sp, rep from *** across to next corner ch-3 sp, ch 3, (dc, picot, 2 dc, picot, 2 dc, picot, dc) in corner ch-3 sp *(corner)*, ****ch 2, (dc, picot, dc) in next ch-3 sp, ch 2, sc in next sp, rep from **** across to beg ch-3, ch 3, join in 3rd ch of beg ch-3. Fasten off. ■

ARAN AFGHAN
Continued from page 30

each of next 3 dc, 2 dc in next sp, [dc in next dc, dc in next sp] twice, dc in next dc, 2 dc in next sp, join in beg sc. Fasten off. *(88 dc)*

ASSEMBLY
Join Motifs tog in 9 rows of 6 Motifs each. To join Motifs, hold 2 Motifs WS tog, working in **back lps** *(see Stitch Guide)* only, sew Motifs tog across 1 side, beg and ending in 4th dc of corners. Join rem Motifs in rows in same manner, then join rows tog.

BORDER
Hold piece with RS facing and 1 short end at top, join yarn with sc in 4th dc of right-hand corner, ch 4, sc in same dc *(corner)*, *ch 3, sk next 2 dc, dc in next dc, **picot** *(see Special Stitches)*, ch 2, sk next dc, (tr, picot,

tr) in next dc, ch 2, sk next dc, dc in next dc, picot, ch 2, sk next 2 dc, sc in next dc, ch 2, sk next 2 dc, dc in next dc, picot, ch 2, sk next dc, (tr, picot, tr) in next dc, ch 2, sk next dc, dc in next dc, picot, ch 3, sc in next joining, picot, rep from * 4 times, ch 2, sk next dc, (tr, picot, tr) in next dc, ch 2, sk next dc, dc in next dc, picot, ch 3, sk next 2 dc, (sc, ch 4, sc) in next dc *(corner)*, **ch 3, sk next 2 dc, dc in next dc, picot, ch 2, sk next dc, (tr, picot, tr) in next dc, ch 2, sk next dc, dc in next dc, picot, ch 2, sk next 2 dc, sc in next dc, ch 2, sk next 2 dc, dc in next dc, picot, ch 2, sk next dc, (tr, picot, tr) in next dc, ch 2, sk next dc, dc in next dc, picot, ch 3, sc in next joining, picot, rep from ** 7 times, ch 2, sk next dc, (tr, picot, tr) in next dc, ch 2, sk next dc, dc in next dc, picot, ch 3, sk next 2 dc, (sc, ch 4, sc) in next dc *(corner)*, ***ch 3, sk next 2 dc, dc in next dc, picot, ch 2, sk next dc, (tr, picot, tr) in next dc, ch 2, sk next dc, dc in next dc, picot, ch 2, sk next 2 dc, sc in next dc, ch 2, sk next 2 dc, dc in next dc, picot, ch 2, sk next dc, (tr, picot, tr) in next dc, ch 2, sk next dc, dc in next dc, picot, ch 3, sc in next joining, picot, rep from *** 4 times, ch 2, sk next dc, (tr, picot, tr) in next dc, ch 2, sk next dc, dc in next dc, picot, ch 3, sk next 2 dc, (sc, ch 4, sc) in next dc *(corner)*, ****ch 3, sk next 2 dc, dc in next dc, picot, ch 2, sk next dc, (tr, picot, tr) in next dc, ch 2, sk next dc, dc in next dc, picot, ch 2, sk next 2 dc, sc in next dc, ch 2, sk next 2 dc, dc in next dc, picot, ch 2, sk next dc, (tr, picot, tr) in next dc, ch 2, sk next dc, dc in next dc, picot, ch 3, sc in next joining, picot, rep from **** 7 times, ch 2, sk next dc, (tr, picot, tr) in next dc, ch 2, sk next dc, dc in next dc, picot, ch 3, sk next 2 dc, join in beg sc. Fasten off. ■

FROSTY LACE
Continued from page 33

Row 4: Ch 5 *(see Pattern Notes)*, sc in ch-1 sp of next V-st, *ch 5, sc in ch-1 sp of next V-st, rep from * across, ch 2, dc in 3rd ch of beg ch-4, turn. *(41 sc, 2 dc, 40 ch-5 sps, 2 ch-2 sps)*

Row 5: Ch 1, sc in first dc, *3 dc in next sc, sc in next ch-5 sp, rep from * across to last sc, 3 dc in last sc, sc in 3rd ch of beg ch-5, turn. *(123 dc, 42 sc)*

Row 6: Ch 3 *(see Pattern Notes)*, sk next dc, sc in next dc, *ch 3, sk next 3 sts, sc in next dc, rep from * across to last 2 sts, ch 1, sk next dc, hdc in last sc, turn. *(2 hdc, 41 sc, 40 ch-3 sps, 2 ch-1 sps)*

Row 7: Ch 3, dc in next ch-1 sp, dc in next sc, *3 dc in next ch-3 sp, dc in next sc, rep from * across to beg ch-3, dc in sp formed by beg ch-3, dc in 2nd ch of same beg ch. *(165 dc)*

Rows 8–115: [Rep rows 2–7 consecutively] 18 times. At end of last row, fasten off.

EDGING
Rnd 1: Hold piece with RS facing and row 115 at top, join yarn with sl st in 3rd ch of beg ch-3 of row 115, ch 1, sc in same st, sc in each dc across *(mark last sc made)*, working across next side in ends of rows, work 191 sc evenly spaced across to row 1 *(mark last sc made)*, working across next side in unused lps of beg ch, sc in each lp across *(mark last sc made)*, working across next side in ends of rows, work 191 evenly spaced across to beg sc, join in beg sc. *(712 sc)*

Rnd 2: Ch 1, 2 sc in same sc *(corner)*, *sc in each sc across to next marked sc, 3 sc in marked sc *(corner)*, rep from * twice, sc in each sc across to same sc as beg 2 sc, sc in same sc, join in beg sc. *(720 sc)*

Rnd 3: Beg large V-st *(see Special Stitches)* in same sc, *sk next 2 sc, **large V-st** *(see Special Stitches)* in next sc, rep from * around, join in 3rd ch of beg ch-5. *(240 V-sts)*

Rnd 4: Sl st in next ch-2 sp, **beg shell** *(see Pattern Notes)* in same sp, *large V-st in ch-2 sp of each large V-st across to next corner, **shell** *(see Pattern Notes)* in ch-2 sp of corner large V-st, rep from * around, join in 3rd ch of beg ch-3. *(236 V-sts, 4 shells)*

Rnd 5: Sl st in next dc, sl st in next ch-2 sp, beg **picot shell** *(see Special Stitches)* in same sp, **picot shell** *(see Special Stitches)* in ch-2 sp of each large V-st and in ch-2 sp of each shell around, join in 3rd ch of beg ch-3. Fasten off. ■

FRENCH STRIPES
Continued from page 34

Side Border
Row 1 (RS): Hold piece with RS facing and 1 long side at top, join dusty blue with sl st in end of first row in upper right corner, ch 1, sc in same sp, work 187 sc evenly spaced across, turn. *(188 sc)*
Row 2: Ch 1, sc in each sc across. Fasten off.
Rep on other long side.

Bottom Border
Row 1 (RS): Hold piece with RS facing and 1 short side at top, join dusty blue with sl st in end of first row in upper right corner, ch 1, sc in same sp, working in ends of rows, work 122 sc evenly spaced across, turn. *(123 sc)*
Row 2: Ch 1, sc in each sc across, turn.
Row 3: Ch 1, sc in each of first 2 sc, *ch 3, sk next 2 sc, **cl** *(see Special Stitches)* in next sc, ch 3, sk next 2 sc, sc in next sc, rep from * across to last sc, sc in last sc, turn. *(20 cl, 21 sc)*
Row 4: Ch 5 *(see Pattern Notes)*, sc in top of next cl, *ch 2, dc in next sc, ch 2, sc in top of next cl, rep from * across to last 2 sc, ch 2, sk next sc, dc in last sc, turn. *(123 sts)*
Row 5: Ch 1, sc in each st and in each ch across, turn. *(123 sc)*
Row 6: Ch 1, sc in each sc, turn.
Row 7: Ch 1, sc in each of first 2 sc, *sk next sc, (hdc, dc, tr) in next sc, **triple picot** *(see*

Special Stitches) in last tr, (tr, dc, hdc) in next sc, sk next sc, sc in each of next 2 sc, rep from * across. Fasten off.
Rep on other short side.

Side Edging
Hold piece with RS facing and 1 long side at top, join dusty blue with sl st in edge of last row in left-hand corner, ch 1, sc in same sp, working left to right, work 8 **reverse sc** *(see Fig. 1)* evenly spaced across border, reverse sc in each sc across to beg of next border, work 8 rev sc evenly spaced across border. Fasten off.
Rep on other long side.

FINISHING
Lightly block afghan as diagonal shell stitch has tendency to bias. ■

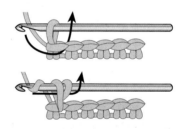

**Reverse Single Crochet
Fig. 1**

LACY CROSS-STITCH
Continued from page 37

Rnd 2: *Sl st in next ch-1 sp, ch 1, rep from * across to next corner ch-2 sp, sl st in corner ch-2 sp, ch 3, **sl st in next sc, ch 3, rep from ** across to next corner ch-2 sp, sl st in corner ch-2 sp, ch 1, ***sl st in next ch-1 sp, ch 1, rep from *** across to next corner ch-2 sp, sl st in corner ch-2 sp, ch 3, ****sl st in next sc, ch 3, rep from **** across to next corner ch-2 sp, sl st in corner ch-2 sp, ch 1, join in beg sl st. Fasten off.

FRINGE

Hold afghan with RS facing and 1 short end at top, join yarn with sc in first ch-3 sp in right-hand corner, ch 25 loosely, sl st in 2nd ch from hook, sl st in each rem ch, ch 1, sc in same sp, *ch 25 loosely, sl st in 2nd ch from hook, sl st in each rem ch, ch 1, sc in next ch-3 sp, ch 25 loosely, sl st in 2nd ch from hook, sl st in each rem ch, ch 1, sc in same sp, rep from * across. Fasten off. Rep on other short end. ■

LACY SQUARES WITH SCALLOPED EDGES

Continued from page 40

sk next ch, sk next sc, ***sc in each of next 9 sc, ch 1, sk next sc, sk next ch, dc in next dc, ch 1, [dc, ch 1] 3 times in next ch-3 sp, dc in next dc, ch 1, sk next ch, sk next sc, rep from *** across to beg sc, join in beg sc.

Rnd 4: Ch 1, sk joined sc, sc in each of next 7 sc, ch 1, sk next sc, sk next ch, *dc in next dc, [ch 2, dc in next dc] 8 times, ch 1, sk next ch, sk next sc, sc in each of next 7 sc, ch 1, sk next sc, sk next ch, **dc in next dc, [ch 2, dc in next dc] 4 times, ch 1, sk next ch, sk next sc, sc in each of next 7 sc, ch 1, sk next sc, sk next ch, rep from ** across to first dc of next corner, rep from * twice, dc in next dc, [ch 2, dc in next dc] 8 times, ch 1, sk next ch, sk next sc, ***sc in each of next 7 sc, ch 1, sk next sc, sk next ch, dc in next dc, [ch 2, dc in next dc] 4 times, ch 1, sk next ch, sk next sc, rep from *** across to beg sc, join in beg sc.

Rnd 5: Ch 1, sk joined sc, sc in next sc, **picot cl** (see Special Stitches), sk next 3 sc, sc in next sc, sk next sc, sk next ch, *dc in next dc, picot cl, [dc in next dc, picot cl] 3 times, [dc in next ch-2 sp, picot cl] twice, [dc in next dc, picot cl] 3 times, dc in next dc, sk next ch, sk next sc, sc in next sc, picot cl, sk next 3 sc, sc in next sc, sk next sc, sk next ch, **[dc in next dc, picot cl] twice, dc in next ch-2 sp, picot cl, dc in next ch-2 sp, [picot cl, dc in next dc] twice, sk next ch, sk next sc, sc in next sc, picot cl, sk next 3 sc, sc in next sc, sk next sc, sk next ch, rep from ** across to first dc of next corner, rep from* twice, dc in next dc, picot cl, [dc in next dc, picot cl] 3 times, [dc in next ch-2 sp, picot cl] twice, [dc in next dc, picot cl] 3 times, dc in next dc, sk next ch, sk next sc, ***sc in next sc, picot cl, sk next 3 sc, sc in next sc, [dc in next dc, picot cl] twice, dc in next ch-2 sp, picot cl, dc in next ch-2 sp, [picot cl, dc in next dc] twice, sk next ch, sk next sc, rep from *** across to beg sc, join in beg sc. Fasten off. ■

Estate Jewel Tones

Brilliant jewel colors like ruby, emerald, sapphire, amethyst, topaz and more make up these gorgeous afghans. Share the wealth as you make these jewels for family and friends.

Jewel Tones Tunisian

Design by Cynthia Adams

SKILL LEVEL

■■■□ INTERMEDIATE

FINISHED SIZE
42 x 52 inches

MATERIALS
• Red Heart Classic medium
  (worsted) weight yarn (Multis:
  3 oz/146 yds/85g per skein):
  8 skeins #959 gemstone
• Size H/8/5mm afghan crochet hook
  or size needed to obtain gauge
• Size I/9/5.5mm crochet hook or
  size needed to obtain gauge
• Tapestry needle

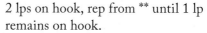

GAUGE
11 vertical bars = 4 inches

PATTERN NOTE
Weave in ends as work progresses.

INSTRUCTIONS

CENTER
Row 1 (RS): With size H afghan hook,
ch 104, insert hook in 3rd ch from hook,
yo, draw lp through, ch 1, *insert hook
in next ch, yo, draw lp through, ch 1, rep
from * across. To work lps off, yo, draw
through 1 lp on hook, **yo, draw through
2 lps on hook, rep from ** until 1 lp
remains on hook.

Row 2: Ch 1, sk first vertical bar, insert
hook under next vertical bar, yo, draw lp
through, ch 1, *insert hook under next vertical
bar, yo, draw lp through, ch 1, rep from *
across, to work lps off, yo, draw through 1 lp
on hook, **yo, draw through 2 lps on hook,
rep from ** until 1 lp remains on hook.
Rep row 2 until piece measures 51 inches
from beg.

Last row: Ch 1, sk first vertical bar, *insert
hook under next vertical bar, yo, draw
through 2 lps on hook, rep from * across.
Do not fasten off.

EDGING
Row 1 (RS): With size I crochet hook,
ch 1, working down next side, 3 sc in first
vertical bar, sc in each edge vertical bar
and in each edge ch-1 sp to last edge
vertical bar, 3 sc in last edge vertical bar,
working across next side in unused lps of
beg ch, sc in each lp across to last lp, 3 sc
in last lp, working across next side, sc in
each edge vertical bar and in each edge
ch-1 sp to last vertical bar, 3 sc in last
vertical bar, turn.
Rnd 2: Ch 1, now working in rnds, sc in
first sc, *ch 3, 2 dc in 3rd ch from hook, sk
next 2 sc, sl st in next sc, rep from * around,
join with sl st in first sc. Fasten off. ■

Treasures of the Deep

Design by Norma Gale

SKILL LEVEL

 INTERMEDIATE

FINISHED SIZE

43 x 55 inches, excluding fringe

MATERIALS

- Red Heart Super Saver medium (worsted) weight yarn (7 oz/ 364 yds/198g per skein):
    3 skeins #512 turqua
    2 skeins each #356 amethyst and #376 burgundy
- Caron Simply Soft medium (worsted) weight yarn (6 oz/330 yds/170g per skein):
    3 skeins #9703 bone
- Size H/8/5mm crochet hook or size needed to obtain gauge
- Tapestry needle

GAUGE

6 sts = 1¾ inches; 6 rows = 1⅞ inches

PATTERN NOTES

Weave in ends as work progresses.

Join with a slip stitch unless otherwise stated.

Chain-5 at beginning of double treble crochet rows counts as first double treble crochet unless otherwise stated.

SPECIAL STITCHES

Cluster (cl): Holding back last lp of each dc on hook, dc in 3 indicated sts, yo and draw through all 4 lps on hook.

Single crochet cluster (sc cl): Draw up lp in each of 3 indicated sts, yo and draw through all 3 lps on hook.

INSTRUCTIONS

PANEL A

Make 7.

CENTER

Row 1: With amethyst, ch 7, sc in 2nd ch from hook and in each rem ch across, turn. *(6 sc)*

Row 2: Ch 1, sc in each sc across, turn.

Rows 3–5: Rep row 2.

Note: Following row completes 1 square and begins next square.

Row 6: Ch 1, sc in each sc across, ch 7, sc in 2nd ch from hook and in next 5 chs, turn.

Rows 7–117: [Rep rows 2–6 consecutively] 22 times.

Rows 118–121: Rep rows 2–5.

Row 122: Ch 1, sc in each st across. Fasten off.

EDGING

Notes: Following rnd will be worked on all sides of squares, working in sts, in ends of rows and in unworked side of beg chs. When working in unworked side of beg chs, insert hook in sts below chs. Be

Continued on page 69

Scraps Spectacular

Design by Martha Brooks Stein

SKILL LEVEL
 EASY

FINISHED SIZE
45 x 56 inches, excluding fringe

MATERIALS
- Red Heart Classic medium (worsted) weight yarn (3½ oz/ 190 yds/99g per skein):
  6 skeins #12 black
- Medium (worsted) weight yarn:
  31 oz/1,550 yds/877g assorted scrap colors
- Size I/9/5.5mm crochet hook or size needed to obtain gauge
- Tapestry needle

GAUGE
Square = 2¾ inches

PATTERN NOTES
Weave in ends as work progresses.

Join with a slip stitch unless otherwise stated.

Chain-2 at beginning of double crochet rounds counts as first double crochet unless otherwise stated.

Chain-4 at beginning of double crochet rounds counts as first double crochet and chain-1 space unless otherwise stated.

INSTRUCTIONS

ONE-SQUARE BLOCK
Make 14.
Rnd 1: With any scrap color, ch 4, join with sl st in first ch to form ring, **ch 2** *(see Pattern Notes)*, 2 dc in ring, ch 2, [3 dc in ring, ch 2] twice, 3 dc in ring, join with hdc in 2nd ch of beg ch-2. *(12 dc, 4 ch-2 sps)*
Rnd 2: Ch 2, 2 dc in sp formed by joining hdc *(beg corner)*, ch 1, *(3 dc, ch 3, 3 dc) in next ch-2 sp *(corner)*, ch 1, rep from * twice, 3 dc in same sp beg ch-2 made, ch 2, **join** in 2nd ch of beg ch-2. Fasten off.
Rnd 3: Join black in any corner ch-3 sp, ch 1, sc in same sp *(beg corner)*, *sc in each of next 3 dc, sc in next ch-1 sp, sc in each of next 3 dc, (sc, ch 2, sc) in next corner ch-3 sp *(corner)*, rep from * twice, sc in each of next 3 dc, sc in next ch-1 sp, sc in each of next 3 dc, sc in next corner ch-3 sp, ch 2, join in beg sc. Fasten off.

TWO-SQUARE BLOCK
Make 119.

Square
Make 2 of same scrap color.
Rnds 1 & 2: Rep rnds 1 & 2 of One-Square Block.

ASSEMBLY
With same scrap color and working in **back lps** *(see Stitch Guide)* only, sew Squares tog across 1 side.

Continued on page 70

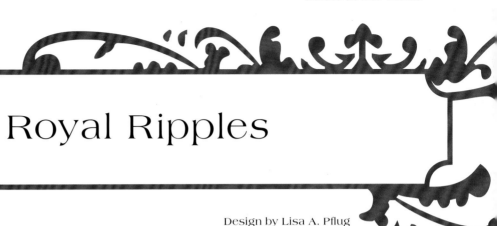

Royal Ripples

Design by Lisa A. Pflug

SKILL LEVEL
 EASY

FINISHED SIZE
44 x 58 inches, excluding tassels

MATERIALS
- Lion Brand Vanna's Choice medium (worsted) weight yarn (3½ oz/170 yds/100g per ball):
    4 balls each #147 purple and #146 dusty grape
    2 balls each #133 brick and #158 mustard
- Size J/10/6mm crochet hook or size needed to obtain gauge
- Tapestry needle

GAUGE
8 dc = 3 inches; 4 dc rows = 3 inches

PATTERN NOTE
Weave in ends as work progresses.

SPECIAL STITCHES
Cluster (cl): Holding back last lp of each dc on hook, dc in 3 indicated sts, yo and draw through all 4 lps on hook.
Single crochet cluster (sc cl): Draw up lp in each of 3 indicated sts, yo and draw through all 3 lps on hook.

INSTRUCTIONS

AFGHAN
Note: On rows worked in front lps only, work first and last st in both lps to give more stability to ends.

Row 1 (RS): With purple, ch 122, working in **back lps** *(see Stitch Guide)* only of chs, dc in 4th ch from hook, dc in each of next 4 chs, *3 dc in next ch, dc in each of next 7 chs, **cl** *(see Special Stitches)* in next 3 chs, dc in each of next 7 chs, rep from * 5 times, 3 dc in next ch, dc in each of last 5 chs, turn. *(6 cl, 115 dc)*

Row 2: Ch 2, dc in each of next 5 sts, *3 dc in next st, dc in each of next 7 sts, cl in next 3 sts, dc in each of next 7 sts, rep from * 5 times, 3 dc in next st, dc in each of next 4 sts, **dc dec** *(see Stitch Guide)* in next 2 sts, **change color** *(see Stitch Guide)* to dusty grape, turn. Fasten off purple. *(6 cl, 115 dc)*

Rows 3 & 4: Rep row 2. At end of row 4, change color to brick. Fasten off dusty grape.

Row 5: Rep row 2, changing color to mustard at end of row. Fasten off brick.

Row 6: Ch 1, sk first st, sc in next st, working in **front lps** *(see Stitch Guide)* only, sc in each of next 4 sts, *3 sc in next st, sc in each of next 7 st, **sc cl** *(see Special Stitches)* in next 3 sts, sc in each of next 7 sts, rep from * 5 times, 3 sc in next st, sc in each of next 4 sts, **sc dec** *(see Stitch Guide)*

Continued on page 71

Rings & Things Afghan

Design by Leshia Tweddle

SKILL LEVEL
■■□□ EASY

FINISHED SIZE
52 x 75 inches

MATERIALS
- Red Heart Soft Yarn medium (worsted) weight yarn (5 oz/ 256 yds/140g per skein):
    4 skeins each #2515 turquoise, #4420 guacamole and #9518 teal
- Berroco Bonsai medium (worsted) weight yarn (1¾ oz/77 yds/50g per skein):
    4 skeins #4121 raku brown
- Size I/9/5.5mm crochet hook or size needed to obtain gauge
- Tapestry needle

GAUGE
1 oval = 2 x 2½ inches

PATTERN NOTES
Weave in ends as work progresses.

Join with a slip stitch unless otherwise stated.

Chain-3 at beginning of double crochet rounds counts as first double crochet unless otherwise stated.

INSTRUCTIONS

STRIP
Make 7 each turquoise, guacamole and teal.

Foundation Row: Ch 6, dtr in 6th ch from hook *(oval)*, *ch 9, dtr in 6th ch from hook *(oval)*, rep from * 28 times, turn. *(30 ovals)*

Rnd 1: Ch 3 *(see Pattern Notes)*, 11 dc in sp formed by next dtr, *sk next ch, sl st in next ch, sk next ch, 12 dc in sp formed by next dtr, rep from * across, on opposite side of foundation row, 12 dc in first ch-6 sp, **sk next ch, sl st in next ch, sk next ch, 12 dc in next ch-6 sp, rep from ** to beg ch-3, join in 3rd ch of beg ch-3. Fasten off.

Continued on page 72

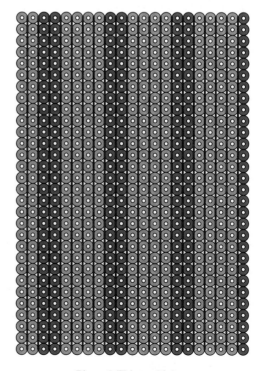

Rings & Things Afghan
Assembly Diagram

Kaleidoscope Afghan

Design by Darla Sims

SKILL LEVEL

 EASY

FINISHED SIZE
61 x 61 inches

MATERIALS
- Red Heart Super Saver medium (worsted) weight yarn (7 oz/ 364 yds/198g per skein):
    2 skeins each #312 black, #776 dark orchid and #656 real teal
    1 skein each #905 magenta and #321 gold
- Sizes H/8/5mm and I/9/5.5mm crochet hooks or size needed to obtain gauge
- Tapestry needle

GAUGE
With size I hook: triangle side = 10 inches

PATTERN NOTES
Weave in ends as work progresses.

Join with a slip stitch unless otherwise stated.

Chain-3 at beginning of double crochet rounds counts as first double crochet unless otherwise stated.

SPECIAL STITCHES
Beginning cluster (beg cl): Ch 2, holding back last lp of each dc on hook, 2 dc in indicated sp, yo and draw through all 3 lps on hook.

Cluster (cl): Holding back last lp of each dc on hook, 3 dc in indicated sp, yo and draw through all 4 lps on hook.

Picot: Ch 5, sl st in top of last st.

INSTRUCTIONS

TRIANGLE
Make 54.

Rnd 1 (RS): With size I hook and magenta, ch 5, join in first ch to form ring, **beg cl** *(see Special Stitches)* in ring, [ch 5, **cl** *(see Special Stitches)*, ch 3, cl] twice in ring, ch 5, cl in ring, ch 3, **join** in top of beg cl. Fasten off. *(6 cl, 3 ch-5 sps, 3 ch-3 sps)*

Rnd 2: Join gold in any ch-5 sp, (beg cl, ch 4, cl, **picot**—*see Special Stitches*, ch 4, cl) in same ch-5 sp, *ch 3, sc in next ch-3 sp, ch 3, (cl, ch 4, cl, picot, ch 4, cl) in next ch-5 sp, rep from * once, ch 3, sc in next ch-3 sp, ch 3, join in top of beg cl. Fasten off. *(9 cl, 3 sc, 6 ch-4 sps, 6 ch-3 sps)*

Rnd 3: Join real teal in any picot, **ch 3** *(see Pattern Notes)*, (dc, ch 5, 2 dc) in same sp, *5 dc in next ch-4 sp, dc in top of next cl, 3 dc in next ch-3 sp, dc in top of next cl, 3 dc in next ch-3 sp, dc in next sc, 5 dc in next ch-5 sp **, (2 dc, ch 5, 2 dc) in next ch-4 sp, rep from * twice, ending last rep at **, join in 3rd ch of beg ch-3. Fasten off. *(6 cl, 3 ch-5 sps, 19 dc)*

Rnd 4: Join dark orchid in any ch-5 sp, (beg cl, ch 3, cl, picot, ch 3, cl) in same sp, *ch 1, sk next dc, [dc in next dc, ch 1, sk

Continued on page 71

Jeweled Octagons

Design by Patricia Kristoffersen

SKILL LEVEL
■■■▶ EXPERIENCED

FINISHED SIZE
47 x 58 inches

MATERIALS
- Medium (worsted) weight yarn: 21 oz/1,050 yds/595g each pink and purple 17 oz/850 yds/482g black
- Size H/8/5mm crochet hook or size needed to obtain gauge
- Tapestry needle

GAUGE
Rnds 1–3 = 3 inches; Octagon = 10¾ inches

PATTERN NOTES
Weave in ends as work progresses.

Join with a slip stitch unless otherwise stated.

Chain-2 at beginning of single crochet rounds counts as first single crochet and chain-1 space unless otherwise stated.

Chain-3 at beginning of double crochet rounds counts as first double crochet unless otherwise stated.

Chain-4 at beginning of single crochet rounds counts as first single crochet and chain-3 space unless otherwise stated.

Chain-4 at beginning of double crochet rounds counts as first double crochet and chain-1 space unless otherwise stated.

SPECIAL STITCHES
Front post treble crochet (fptr): Yo twice, insert hook from front to back to front around **post** *(see Stitch Guide)* of indicated st, yo, draw lp through, [yo, draw through 2 lps on hook] 3 times.

Front post double treble crochet (fpdtr): Yo 3 times, insert hook from front to back to front around **post** *(see Stitch Guide)* of indicated st, yo, draw lp through, [yo, draw through 2 lps on hook] 4 times.

Cluster (cl): Holding back last lp of each **fpdtr** *(see Special Stitches)* on hook, fpdtr around indicated st, sk next fptr, fpdtr around next fptr, yo and draw through all 3 lps on hook.

Large cluster (large cl): Holding back last lp of each st on hook, tr indicated front lp, sk next front lp, dc in each of next 2 front lps, sk next front lp, tr in next front lp, yo and draw through all 5 lps on hook.

Front post double crochet cluster (fpdc cl): Holding back last lp of each fpdc on hook, fpdtr around each of 2 indicated sts, yo and draw through all 3 lps on hook.

INSTRUCTIONS

PINK OCTAGON
Make 10.
Rnd 1 (RS): With pink, ch 6, join to form ring, ch 2, 18 dc in ring, **join** in first dc. *(18 dc)*

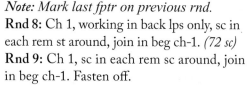

Rnd 2: Ch 2 *(see Pattern Notes),* [sc in next dc, ch 1] 17 times, join in first ch of beg ch-2. *(18 sc, 18 ch-1 sps)*

Rnd 3: Sl st in next ch-1 sp, **ch 4** *(see Pattern Notes),* [sc in next ch-1 sp, ch 3] 17 times, join in first ch of beg ch-4. Fasten off. *(18 sc, 18 ch-3 sps)*

Rnd 4: Join purple with sc in last ch-3 sp of previous rnd, **fptr** *(see Special Stitches)* around first dc on rnd 1, sc in next ch-3 sp on previous rnd, [fptr around next dc on rnd 1, sc in next ch-3 sp on previous rnd] 16 times, fptr around last dc on rnd 1, join in **back lp** *(see Stitch Guide)* of beg sc. *(18 fptr, 18 sc)*

Note: Mark 2nd fptr on previous rnd.

Rnd 5: Ch 1 *(does not count as a st),* sc in same lp as joining, working in back lps only, [sc in next fptr, 2 sc in next sc] 17 times, sc in last fptr, join in beg ch-1. *(54 sc)*

Rnd 6: Ch 1, sc in each rem sc around, join in beg ch-1. Fasten off.

Rnd 7: Join pink in same sc as joining of previous rnd, ch 1, sc in next sc, fptr around marked fptr on rnd 4, [sc in each of next 3 sc, fptr around next fptr on rnd 4] 17 times, sc in last sc, join in beg ch-1. *(18 fptr, 54 sc)*

Note: Mark last fptr on previous rnd.

Rnd 8: Ch 1, working in back lps only, sc in each rem st around, join in beg ch-1. *(72 sc)*

Rnd 9: Ch 1, sc in each rem sc around, join in beg ch-1. Fasten off.

Rnd 10: Join purple in same ch as joining of previous rnd, ch 1, sc in next sc, fptr around marked fpdc on rnd 7, [sc in each of next 4 sc, fptr around next fpdc on rnd 7] 17 times, sc in each of last 2 sc, join in beg ch-1. *(18 fptr, 72 sc)*

Note: Mark last fptr on previous rnd.

Rnds 11 & 12: Rep rnd 8. At end of rnd 12, fasten off.

Rnd 13: Join pink with sc in same sc as joining of previous rnd, sc in next sc, **cl** *(see Special Stitches)* around marked fptr on rnd 10 and next 2 fptr, sk sc on previous rnd behind cl, [sc in next 4 sc, cl around next 3 fptr on rnd 10, sk sc on previous rnd behind cl] 17 times, sc in each of last 2 sc, join in beg sc. *(18 cl, 72 sc)*

Rnd 14: Ch 1, sc in next sc, [2 sc in next cl, sc in each of next 4 sc] 17 times, 2 sc in next cl, sc in each of last 2 sc, join in beg ch-1. *(108 sc)*

Rnd 15: Ch 1, sc in each of next 25 sc, [2 sc in next sc, sc in each of next 26 sc] 3 times, 2 sc in next sc, join in beg ch-1. Fasten off. *(112 sc)*

Rnd 16: Join black in back lp of any sc, **ch 2** *(see Pattern Notes),* (dc, hdc) in same sc *(beg corner),* *hdc in each of next 5 sc, sc in each of next 3 sc, hdc in each of next 5 sc, (hdc, dc, hdc) in next sc *(corner),* rep from * 6 times, hdc in each of next 5 sc, sc in each of next 3 sc, hdc in each of next 5 sc, join in 2nd ch of beg ch-2. *(128 sts)*

Rnd 17: Ch 1, [2 sc in next st *(corner),* sc in each of next 15 sts] 7 times, 2 sc in next st *(corner),* sc in each of next 14 sts, join in beg ch-1. Fasten off. *(136 sc)*

PURPLE OCTAGON
Make 10.

Work same as Pink Octagon, reversing colors.

SQUARE

Make 12.

Rnd 1 (RS): With black, ch 5, join to form ring, **ch 3** *(see Pattern Notes)*, 11 dc in ring, join in 3rd ch of beg ch-3. *(12 dc)*

Rnd 2: **Ch 2,** [sc in next dc, ch 1] 11 times, join in first ch of beg ch-2. *(12 sc, 12 ch-1 sps)*

Rnd 3: Sl st in next ch-1 sp, **ch 4** , [sc in next ch-1 sp, ch 3] 11 times, join in first ch of beg ch-4. Fasten off.

Rnd 4: Join pink in any ch-3 sp, 3 sc in same sp, *[fptr around next dc on rnd 1, sc in next ch-3 sp] twice, fptr around next dc on rnd 1 **, 3 sc in next ch-3 sp, rep from * 3 times, ending last rep at **, join in beg sc. *Note: Mark 2nd fptr of each 3-fptr group on previous rnd.*

Rnd 5: Ch 1, [3 sc in next sc, sc in each of next 7 sts] 3 times, 3 sc in next sc, sc in each of last 6 sts, join in beg ch-1. Fasten off.

Rnd 6: Join purple in same ch as joining of previous rnd, ch 1, sc in next sc, 3 sc in next sc *(corner)*, sc in each of next 2 sc, fptr around marked fptr on rnd 4, sc in each of next 5 sc, fptr around same fptr on rnd 4, sc in each of next 2 sc, *3 sc in next sc *(corner)*, sc in each of next 2 sc, fptr around next marked fptr on rnd 4, sc in each of next 5 sc, fptr around same fptr **, sc in each of next 2 sc, rep from * twice, ending last rep at **, join in beg ch-1. Fasten off.

Rnd 7: Join black in first sc of any corner, ch 1, 3 sc in next sc *(corner)*, sc in each of next 3 sc, **fpdtr** *(see Special Stitches)* around 3rd fptr of last 3-fptr group on rnd 4, sk next fptr on previous rnd, sc in each of next 5 sc, sk next fptr, fpdtr around first fptr of next 3-fptr group on rnd 4, sc in each of next 3 sc, rep from * 3 times, ending last rep at **, sc in each of last 2 sc, join in beg ch-1.

Rnd 8: Ch 1, working in back lps only, ch 1, sc in next st, [2 sc in next st *(corner)*, sc in each of next 15 sts] 3 times, 2 sc in next st *(corner)*, sc in each of next 13 sts, join in beg ch-1. Fasten off.

ASSEMBLY

Referring to diagram, join Octagons in 5 rows of 4 Octagons each. With black and working in back lps only, sl st corresponding sides of Octagons tog, beg in first corner sc and ending in last corner sc of sides. Join Squares in same manner.

Jeweled Octagons
Assembly Diagram

BORDER

Rnd 1: Hold piece with 1 short end at top, join black in first sc of first 2-sc corner at top of Octagon in right-hand corner, **ch 4** *(see Pattern Notes)*, dc in each of next 17 sts, ch 1, *dc in each of next 16 sts, sk next st, sk joining, sk next st on next Octagon, dc in each of next 16 sts, ch 1, dc in each of next 17 sts, ch 1, rep from * twice, [dc in each of next 17 sts, ch 1] twice, **dc in each of next 16 sts, sk next st, sk joining, sk next st on next Octagon, dc in each of next 16 sts, ch 1, dc in each of next 17 sts, ch 1, rep from ** 3 times, [dc in each of next 17 sts, ch 1] twice, ***dc in each of next 16 sts, sk next st, sk joining, sk next st on next Octagon, dc in each of next 16 sts, ch 1, dc in each of next 17 sts, ch 1, rep from *** twice, [dc in each of

Continued on page 72

Diagonal Jewels

Design by Delma Myers

SKILL LEVEL

■■■□ INTERMEDIATE

FINISHED SIZE
48 x 64 inches

MATERIALS
- Red Heart Soft Yarn medium (worsted) weight yarn (5 oz/ 256 yds/140g per skein):
  3 skeins each #4614 black, #9518 teal, #2515 turquoise, #3729 grape and #9537 fuchsia
- Sizes G/6/4mm and H/8/5mm crochet hooks or size needed to obtain gauge
- Tapestry needle

GAUGE
With size H hook: 17 sc = 4 inches
Square = 7½ inches square

PATTERN NOTES
Weave in ends as work progresses.

Join with a slip stitch unless otherwise stated.

INSTRUCTIONS

SQUARE
Make 48.
Row 1 (RS): With size H hook and turquoise, ch 6, dc in 4th ch from hook, dc in each of next 2 chs, turn.
Row 2: Ch 6, dc in 4th ch from hook, dc in each of next 2 chs, sl st in sp formed by beg 3 sk chs of previous row, ch 3, 3 dc in same sp, turn.
Row 3: Ch 6, dc in 4th ch from hook, dc in each of next 2 chs, (sl st, ch 3, 3 dc) in each of next 2 ch-3 sps, turn.
Row 4: Ch 6, dc in 4th ch from hook, dc in each of next 2 chs, [(sl st, ch 3, 3 dc) in next ch-3 sp] 3 times. Fasten off. Turn.
Row 5: Join teal in first dc, ch 6, dc in 4th ch from hook, dc in each of next 2 chs, [(sl st, ch 3, 3 dc) in next ch-3 sp] 4 times, turn.
Row 6: Ch 6, dc in 4th ch from hook, dc in each of next 2 chs, [(sl st, ch 3, 3 dc) in next ch-3 sp] 5 times, turn.
Row 7: Ch 6, dc in 4th ch from hook, dc in each of next 2 chs, [(sl st, ch 3, 3 dc) in next ch-3 sp] 6 times, turn.
Row 8: Ch 6, dc in 4th ch from hook, dc in each of next 2 chs, [(sl st, ch 3, 3 dc) in next ch-3 sp] 7 times. Fasten off. Turn.
Row 9: Join black in first dc, ch 6, dc in 4th ch from hook, dc in each of next 2 chs, [(sl st, ch 3, 3 dc) in next ch-3 sp] 8 times, turn.
Row 10: Ch 6, dc in 4th ch from hook, dc in each of next 2 chs, (sl st, ch 3, 3 dc) in next ch-3 sp] 9 times, turn.
Row 11: Sl st in each of first 3 dc and in next ch, ch 3, 3 dc in ch-3 sp, [(sl st, ch 3, 3 dc) in next ch-3 sp] 9 times. Fasten off. Turn.
Row 12: Sk first 3 dc, join grape in next ch, ch 3, 3 dc in ch-3 sp, (sl st, ch 3, 3 dc) in next ch-3 sp] 8 times, turn.
Row 13: Sl st in each of first 3 dc and in next ch, ch 3, 3 dc in ch-3 sp, [(sl st, ch 3, 3 dc) in next ch-3 sp] 7 times, turn.

Row 14: Sl st in each of first 3 dc and in next ch, ch 3, 3 dc in ch-3 sp, [(sl st, ch 3, 3 dc) in next ch-3 sp] 6 times, turn.

Row 15: Sl st in each of first 3 dc and in next ch, ch 3, 3 dc in ch-3 sp, [(sl st, ch 3, 3 dc) in next ch-3 sp] 5 times. Fasten off. Turn.

Row 16: Sk first 3 dc, join fuchsia in next ch, ch 3, 3 dc in ch-3 sp, [(sl st, ch 3, 3 dc) in next ch-3 sp] 4 times, turn.

Row 17: Sl st in each of first 3 dc and in next ch, ch 3, 3 dc in ch-3 sp, [(sl st, ch 3, 3 dc) in next ch-3 sp] 3 times, turn.

Row 18: Sl st in each of first 3 dc and in next ch, ch 3, 3 dc in ch-3 sp, [(sl st, ch 3, 3 dc) in next ch-3 sp] twice, turn.

Row 19: Sl st in each of first 3 dc and in next ch, ch 3, 3 dc in ch-3 sp, [(sl st, ch 3, 3 dc) in next ch-3 sp, turn.

Row 20: Sl st in each of first 3 dc and in next ch, ch 3, 3 dc in ch-3 sp. Fasten off.

ASSEMBLY

Referring to diagram for placement, sew Squares tog in 8 rows of 6 Squares each. To join Squares, place 2 Squares side by side. With tapestry needle, join matching yarn in first edge st on first Square, weave needle through corresponding edge st on 2nd Square, then weave needle through next edge st on first Square, continue in same manner across side. Join rem Squares in same manner.

BORDER

Rnd 1: With size H hook, join black with sc in any corner, 2 sc in same sp, sc in each dc and 2 sc in each sp formed by edge dc and with 3 sc in each corner around, **join** in beg sc. Fasten off.

Rnd 2: Join black in 2nd sc of a different corner, 3 sc in same sc, *sc in each sc to 2nd sc of next corner, 3 sc in 2nd sc, rep from * twice, sc in each sc to beg sc, join in beg sc. Fasten off.

Rnds 3–5: Rep rnd 2. At end of rnd 5, **do not fasten off**.

Rnd 6: With size G hook and working left to right, work reverse sc *(see Fig. 1)* in each sc around, join in beg reverse sc. Fasten off. ∎

Diagonal Jewels
Assembly Diagram

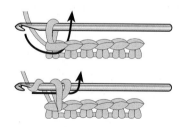

Reverse Single Crochet
Fig. 1

TRASURES OF THE DEEP
Continued from page 53

careful not to twist Panel while working.
Rnd 1 (RS): Hold piece with RS facing and first square made to right, join bone in end of row 2 of first square, ch 1, sc in same sp and in end of each of next 3 rows, 3 sc in next corner, *working across next side, sk first st, sc in each of next 4 sts, sk last st, on next square, sk first st, sc in each of next 4 sts, 3 sc in next corner, rep from * across to last square, sc in each of next 4 sts, 3 sc in next corner, working across next long edge, sc in each of next 4 sts, 3 sc in next corner, **working across next side, sk first st, sc in each of next 4 sts, sk last st, on next square, sk first st, sc in each of next 4 sts, 3 sc in next corner, rep from ** across to last square, sc in each of next 4 sts, 3 sc in next corner, join in beg sc. Fasten off.
Row 2: Hold piece with RS facing, now working in rows, join turqua in 3rd sc of last corner 3-sc group on rnd 1, **ch 5** *(see Pattern Notes)*, 2 dtr in same sc, sk next 4 sc, sc in next sc, *sk next 4 sc, 6 dtr in sp between next 2 sc at bottom of squares, sk next 5 sc, sc in next sc, rep from * 22 times, sk next 5 sc, 3 dtr in next sc. Fasten off. Hold piece with RS facing and opposite long edge at top, join turqua in 3rd sc of first corner 3-sc group at right edge, ch 5, 2 dtr in same sc, sk next 4 sc, sc in next sc, *sk next 4 sc, 6 dtr in sp between next 2 sc at bottom of squares, sk next 5 sc, sc in next sc, rep from * 22 times, sk next 5 sc, 3 dtr in next sc. Fasten off.
Note: There should be 1 unworked sc at each end of Panel.

PANEL B
Make 7.

CENTER
With burgundy, work same as Center of Panel A.

Edging
Work same as Edging of Panel A.

ASSEMBLY
With turqua and tapestry needle and working in **back lps** *(see Stitch Guide)* only, sewing Panels tog, alternating colors.

BORDERS
Side Borders
Row 1 (RS): Hold piece with RS facing and 1 long edge at top, join bone in first st in right-hand corner, ch 1, sc in each st across, turn.
Row 2: Sl st in each st. Fasten off.
Rep rows 1 and 2 on opposite long edge.

Top & Lower Borders
Row 1 (RS): Hold piece with RS facing and 1 short edge at top, join bone in end of edging row in right-hand corner, ch 1, sc in same sp, working across side, work 5 sc in sp formed by each edge dtr, 2 sc in unworked sc at tip of each Panel Center, sc in each Panel joining and sc in end of edging row at opposite end, turn.
Row 2: Sl st in each st. Fasten off.
Rep rows 1 and 2 on opposite short edge.

FRINGE
Cut 14-inch lengths of bone. For each knot of fringe, fold 2 strands in half. From RS, draw folded end through first st at 1 short end of afghan. Draw ends through fold and tighten knot. Place knots in each st across both short ends of afghan. Trim ends evenly. ∎

SCRAPS SPECTACULAR
Continued from page 54

Edging

Hold piece with RS facing and 1 short end at top, join black in right-hand corner ch-3 sp, ch 1, (sc, ch 2, sc) in same sp, sc in each of next 3 dc, sc in next ch-1 sp, sc in each of next 3 dc, (sc, ch 2, sc) in next corner, working across next side, sc in each dc, in each ch sp and in Square joining across to next corner, (sc, ch 2, sc) in corner, working across next side, sc in each dc and in each ch sp across to next corner, (sc, ch 2, sc) in corner, working across next side, sc in each dc, in each ch sp and in Square joining across to beg sc, join in beg sc. Fasten off.

ASSEMBLY

Referring to Assembly Diagram for placement, arrange Blocks. With black and working in back lps only, sew Blocks tog.

BORDER

Rnd 1: Hold piece with RS facing and 1 short end at top, join black in left-hand corner ch-2 sp, ch 1, sc in same sp, *ch 1, sk next sc, sc in next sc, rep from * across to next corner ch-2 sp, (sc, ch 1, sc, ch 1, sc) in corner ch-2 sp *(corner)*, **ch 1, sk next sc, sc in next sc, rep from ** across to next corner ch-2 sp, (sc, ch 1, sc, ch 1, sc) in corner ch-2 sp *(corner)*, ***ch 1, sk next sc, sc in next sc, rep from *** across to next corner ch-2 sp, (sc, ch 1, sc, ch 1, sc) in corner ch-2 sp *(corner)*, ****ch 1, sk next sc, sc in next sc, rep from **** across to next corner ch-2 sp, sc in same sp as beg sc made, join with hdc in beg sc.
Note: Following row is worked on sides of piece only.
Row 2: Now working in rows, *ch 2, sl st in next ch-1 sp, rep from * across to next corner, ch 1, sl st in first ch-1 of corner.
Fasten off.
Join black in 2nd ch-1 sp of lower right-hand corner of right-hand side, *ch 2, sl st in next ch-1 sp, rep from * across side to next corner, ch 1, sl st in first ch-1 of corner. Fasten off.

FRINGE

Cut 22-inch lengths of black. For each knot of fringe, fold 3 lengths in half, draw folded end through first ch-1 sp on 1 short end of afghan. Pull ends through fold and tighten knot. Tie knot in each ch-1 sp across each short end of afghan. Trim ends evenly. ∎

Scraps Spectacular
Assembly Diagram

ROYAL RIPPLES
Continued from page 57

in last 2 sts, change color to purple, turn. Fasten off mustard. *(6 cl, 115 sc)*

Row 7: Working in front lps only, rep row 2.

Rows 8–12: Rep rows 2–6.

Rows 13–72: [Rep rows 7–12 consecutively] 10 times.

Row 73 & 74: Rep rows 7 and 8.

Row 75: Working through both lps, rep row 6. At end of row, fasten off.

Lower Edging
Hold piece with WS facing, and beg ch at top, working in unused lps of beg ch, join purple in first ch in right-hand corner, ch 1, sc in next ch, sc in each of next 4 chs, *3 sc in next ch, sc in each of next 7 chs, sc cl in next 3 chs, sc in each of next 7 chs, rep from * 5 times, 3 sc in next ch, sc in each of next 4 chs, sc dec in last 2 chs. Fasten off.

TASSELS

Cut 17-inch lengths of mustard. For each Tassel, use 14 strands. With hook, pull strands through 2nd sc of first 3-sc group on 1 short end of afghan, having ends meet. Cut 16-inch strand of brick. With brick strand, secure Tassel 1 inch below fold. To do this, wrap yarn tightly around tassel, covering beg of strand, until 3 inches of strand remains. Thread rem length in tapestry needle and insert needle through center of wrapped section to secure.

Place 1 Tassel in center sc of each 3-sc group along top and bottom of afghan. On bottom, also place Tassel in first and last st. ■

KALEIDOSCOPE AFGHAN
Continued from page 61

Kaleidoscope Afghan
Assembly Diagram

next dc] 11 times **, (cl, ch 3, cl, picot, ch 3, cl) in next ch-5 sp, rep from * twice, ending last rep at **, join in top of beg cl. Fasten off. *(9 cl, 33 dc, 6 ch-3 sps, 12 ch-1sps)*

Rnd 5: Join black with sc in any picot, 4 sc in same sp, *3 sc in next ch-3 sp, sc in each st and in each ch-1 sp across to next ch-3 sp, 3 sc in next ch-3 sp **, 5 sc in next picot, rep from * twice, ending last rep at **, join in beg sc. Fasten off. *(117 sc)*

ASSEMBLY
With tapestry needle and black, sew Triangles tog, working through **back lps** *(see Stitch Guide)* only, following diagram.

EDGING

Rnd 1: With size H hook, join black with sc in any st, sc in each st around, working 3 dc in each corner or point; join in beg sc.

Rnd 2: Ch 1, working left to right, work **reverse sc** *(see Fig. 1)* in each sc around; join in first reverse sc. Fasten off. ■

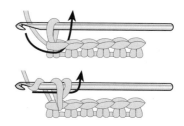

Reverse Single Crochet
Fig. 1

RINGS & THINGS AFGHAN
Continued from page 58

ASSEMBLY

Referring to diagram on page 54 for color placement, arrange Strips. With brown, make slip knot on hook, insert hook in 6th dc on first oval of first Strip and in 6th dc on first oval on 2nd strips, join, ch 1, insert hook in next dc on first oval of first Strip and in next dc on 2nd Strip and join, ch 8, working across Strips, rep joining process in 6th and 7th dc on rem ovals on Strips. Fasten off. Join rem strips in same manner. ■

JEWELED OCTAGONS
Continued from page 65

next 16 sts, ch 1] twice, ****dc in each of next 16 sts, sk next st, sk joining, sk next st on next Octagon, dc in each of next 16 sts, ch 1, dc in each of next 17 sts, ch 1, rep from **** twice, dc in each of next 16 sts, ch 1, join in 3rd ch of beg ch-4.

Note: Mark 3rd ch-1 sp on previous rnd.

Rnd 2: Join pink with sc in marked ch-1 sp on previous rnd, *[tr in **front lp** *(see Stitch Guide)*, of next st on last rnd of Octagon, sc in next st on previous rnd] 8 times, tr in front lp of next st on last rnd of Octagon, sc in next ch-1 sp on previous rnd, [tr in front lp of next st on last rnd of Octagon, sc in next st on previous rnd] 7 times, tr in front lp of next st on last rnd of Octagon, **sc dec** *(see Stitch Guide)* in next 2 dc on previous rnd, [tr in front lp of next st on last rnd of Octagon, sc in next st on previous rnd] 7 times, tr in front lp of next st on last rnd of Octagon, sc in next ch-1 sp on previous rnd, rep from * once, [tr in front lp of next st on last rnd of Octagon, sc in next st on previous rnd] 8 times, [tr in front lp of next st on last rnd of Octagon, sc in next ch-1 sp on previous rnd] 3 times, [tr in front lp of next st on last rnd of Octagon, sc in next st on previous rnd] 7 times, tr in front lp of next st on last rnd of Octagon, sc dec in next 2 dc, [tr in front lp of next st on last rnd of Octagon, sc in next st on previous rnd] 7 times, tr in front lp of next st on last rnd of Octagon, sc in next ch-1 sp, **[tr in front lp, of next st on last rnd of Octagon, sc in next st on previous rnd] 8 times, tr in front lp of next st on last rnd of Octagon, sc in next ch-1 sp on previous rnd, [tr in front

lp of next st on last rnd of Octagon, sc in next st on previous rnd] 7 times, tr in front lp of next st on last rnd of Octagon, sc dec in next 2 dc on previous rnd, [tr in front lp of next st on last rnd of Octagon, sc in next st on previous rnd] 7 times, tr in front lp of next st on last rnd of Octagon, sc in next ch-1 sp on previous rnd, rep from ** twice, [tr in front lp of next st on last rnd of Octagon, sc in next st on previous rnd] 8 times, [tr in front lp of next st on last rnd of Octagon, sc in next ch-1 sp on previous rnd] 3 times, ***[tr in front lp of next st on last rnd of Octagon, sc in next st on previous rnd] 8 times, tr in front lp of next st on last rnd of Octagon, sc in next ch-1 sp on previous rnd, [tr in front lp of next st on last rnd of Octagon, sc in next st on previous rnd] 7 times, tr in front lp of next st on last rnd of Octagon, sc dec in next 2 dc on previous rnd, [tr in front lp of next st on last rnd of Octagon, sc in next st on previous rnd] 7 times, tr in front lp of next st on last rnd of Octagon, sc in next ch-1 sp on previous rnd, rep from *** once, [tr in front lp of next st on last rnd of Octagon, sc in next st on previous rnd] 8 times, [tr in front lp of next st on last rnd of Octagon, sc in next ch-1 sp on previous rnd] 3 times, [tr in front lp of next st on last rnd of Octagon, sc in next st on previous rnd] 7 times, tr in front lp of next st on last rnd of Octagon, sc dec in next 2 dc on previous rnd, [tr in front lp of next st on last rnd of Octagon, sc in next st on previous rnd] 7 times, tr in front lp of next st on last rnd of Octagon, sc in next ch-1 sp on previous rnd, ****[tr in front lp, of next st on last rnd of Octagon, sc in next st on previous rnd] 8 times, tr in front lp of next st on last rnd of Octagon, sc in next ch-1 sp on previous rnd, [tr in front lp of next st on last rnd of Octagon, sc in next st on previous rnd] 7 times, tr in front lp of next st on last rnd of Octagon, sc dec in next 2 dc on previous rnd, [tr in front lp of next st on last rnd of Octagon, sc in next st on previous rnd] 7 times, tr in front lp of next st on last rnd

of Octagon, sc in next ch-1 sp on previous rnd, rep from **** twice, [tr in front lp of next st on last rnd of Octagon, sc in next st on previous rnd] 8 times, [tr in front lp of next st on last rnd of Octagon, sc in next ch-1 sp on previous rnd] 3 times, [tr in front lp of next st on last rnd of Octagon, sc in next st on previous rnd] 7 times, tr in front lp of next st on last rnd of Octagon, sc dec in next 2 dc on previous rnd, [tr in front lp of next st on last rnd of Octagon, sc in next st on previous rnd] 7 times, tr in front lp of next st on last rnd of Octagon, join in beg sc. Fasten off.

Rnd 3: Join purple with sc in last tr made on previous rnd, tr in each of same 2 front lps as next 2 tr, sk corner sc in back, [sc in next st on previous rnd, tr in unused front lp of next st on last rnd of Octagon, sk st in back] 8 times, sc in next st, tr in each of same 2 front lps as next 2 tr, sk corner sc in back, [tr in front lp of next st on last rnd of Octagon, sc in next st] 7 times, **large cl** *(see Special Stitches)* in next 5 front lps, [tr in next unused front lp on last rnd of Octagon, sc in next st on previous rnd] 7 times, tr in each of same 2 front lps as next 2 sts, continue in same manner around, join in beg sc. Fasten off.

Rnd 4: Join black with sc in first tr of previous rnd, ch 1, sc in next st, [fpdc around next tr on rnd 2, sc in next st on previous rnd] 9 times, ch 1, sc in next st on previous rnd, [fpdc around next tr on rnd 2, sc in next st on previous rnd] 7 times, fpdc around next tr on rnd 2, **fpdc cl** *(see Special Stitches)* around next 2 tr on rnd 2, [sc in next tr on previous rnd, fpdc around next tr on rnd 2] 7 times, sc in next st, ch 1, sc in next st, continue in same manner around, join in beg sc.

Note: Push fpdc to top of posts of sts.

Rnd 5: Ch 1, working in back lps only, 2 sc in next ch-1 sp, sc in each of next 19 sts, 2 sc in next ch-1 sp, sc in each of next 14 sts, sk next 3 sts, sc in each of next 14 sts, 2 sc in next ch-1 sp, rep around, join in beg ch-1. Fasten off. ∎

Pineapples & Filets

The pineapple and filet designs have long been favorites with crocheters. You'll find beautiful designs that will make stunning additions to your home or gifts to give.

Pineapple Connection

Design by JoHanna Dzikowski

SKILL LEVEL
 EASY

FINISHED SIZE
37 x 64 inches

MATERIALS
- Red Heart Super Saver medium (worsted) weight yarn (7 oz/ 364 yds/198g per skein): 4 skeins #313 aran
- Size I/9/5.5mm crochet hook or size needed to obtain gauge
- Tapestry needle

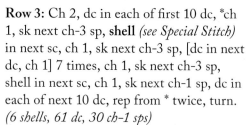

GAUGE
3 dc = 1 inch; 4 rows = 4 inches

PATTERN NOTE
Weave in ends as work progresses.

SPECIAL STITCH
Shell: (2 dc, ch 1, 2 dc) in indicated st.

INSTRUCTIONS

CENTER
Row 1 (RS): Ch 97, sc in 2nd ch from hook, sc in each rem ch across, turn. *(96 sc)*

Row 2: Ch 2, dc in each of first 10 sc, *ch 3, sk next 3 sc, sc in next sc, ch 3, sk next 5 sc, 7 dc in next sc *(base of pineapple)*, ch 3, sk next 5 sc, sc in next sc, ch 3, sk next 3 sc, dc in each of next 10 sc, rep from * twice, turn. *(3 pineapple bases, 40 dc, 6 sc, 12 ch-3 sps)*

Row 3: Ch 2, dc in each of first 10 dc, *ch 1, sk next ch-3 sp, **shell** *(see Special Stitch)* in next sc, ch 1, sk next ch-3 sp, [dc in next dc, ch 1] 7 times, ch 1, sk next ch-3 sp, shell in next sc, ch 1, sk next ch-1 sp, dc in each of next 10 dc, rep from * twice, turn. *(6 shells, 61 dc, 30 ch-1 sps)*

Row 4: Ch 2, dc in each of first 10 dc, *ch 1, sk next ch-1 sp, shell in ch-1 sp of next shell, ch 2, sk next ch-1 sp, sk next dc, [sc in next ch-1 sp, ch 3] 5 times, sc in next ch-1 sp, ch 2, sk next ch-1 sp, shell in ch-1 sp of next shell, ch 1, sk next ch-1 sp, dc in each of next 10 dc, rep from * twice, turn. *(6 shells, 40 dc, 18 sc, 15 ch-3 sps, 6 ch-2 sps, 6 ch-1 sps)*

Row 5: Ch 2, dc in each of first 10 dc, *ch 1, shell in ch-1 sp of next shell, ch 3, sk next ch-2 sp, [sc in next ch-3 sp, ch 3] 4 times, sc in next ch-3 sp, ch 3, sk next ch-2 sp, shell in ch-1 sp of next shell, ch 1, sk next ch-1 sp, dc in each of next 10 dc, rep from * twice, turn. *(6 shells, 40 dc, 15 sc, 18 ch-3 sps, 6 ch-1 sps)*

Row 6: Ch 2, dc in each of first 10 dc, *ch 1, shell in ch-1 sp of next shell, ch 3, sk next ch-3 sp, [sc in next ch-3 sp, ch 3] 3 times, sc in next ch-3 sp, ch 3, sk next ch-3 sp, shell in ch-1 sp of next shell, ch 1, sk next ch-1 sp, dc in each of next 10 dc, rep from * twice, turn. *(6 shells, 40 dc, 12 sc, 15 ch-3 sps, 6 ch-1 sps)*

Row 7: Ch 2, dc in each of first 10 dc, *ch 1, shell in ch-1 sp of next shell, ch 4,

Continued on page 95

Heritage Filet

Design by Norma Gale

SKILL LEVEL

◼◼◼◻ INTERMEDIATE

FINISHED SIZE

51 x 61 inches

MATERIALS

- Red Heart Super Saver medium (worsted) weight yarn (7 oz/ 364 yds/198g per skein):
    3 skeins #312 black
    2 skeins each #334 buff,
    #327 light coral and #512 turqua
- Size F/5/3.75mm crochet hook or size needed to obtain gauge
- Tapestry needle

GAUGE

4 sc = 1 inch; 3 sc rows = 1 inch; [ch 2, sk next ch-2 sp, dc in next sc, ch 2)] 4 times = 3 inches

PATTERN NOTES

Afghan is worked lengthwise.

Weave in ends as work progresses.

Chain-3 at beginning of double crochet rows counts as first double crochet unless otherwise stated.

Chain-5 at beginning of double crochet rows counts as first double crochet and chain-2 space unless otherwise stated.

SPECIAL STITCHES

Beginning popcorn (beg pc): Ch 3, 3 dc in indicated sp, drop lp from hook, insert hook in 3rd ch of beg ch-3, draw dropped lp through.

Popcorn (pc): 4 dc in indicated sp, drop lp from hook, insert hook in first dc, draw dropped lp through.

INSTRUCTIONS

CENTER

Row 1 (WS): With black, ch 245, sc in 2nd ch from hook, sc in each rem ch across, turn. *(244 sc)*

Row 2 (RS): Ch 1, sc in each sc, turn.

Row 3: Ch 1, sc in each sc, **change color** *(see Stitch Guide)* in last sc to light coral, turn. Fasten off black.

Row 4: Ch 3 *(see Pattern Notes)*, *dc in each of next 12 sc, [ch 2, sk next 2 sc, dc in next sc] 4 times, rep from * across to last 3 sc, dc in each of last 3 sc, turn.

Row 5: Ch 5 *(see Pattern Notes)*, sk next 2 dc, dc in next dc, [ch 2, sk next ch-2 sp, dc in next dc] twice, *[2 dc in next ch-2 sp, dc in next dc] twice, dc in each of next 6 dc, [ch 2, sk next 2 dc, dc in next dc] 4 times, rep from * 8 times, [2 dc in next ch-2 sp, dc in next dc] twice, dc in each of next 6 dc, [ch 2, sk next 2 dc, dc in next dc] twice, turn.

Row 6: Ch 5, sk next ch-2 sp, dc in next dc, ch 2, sk next ch-2 sp, dc in next dc, *[ch 2, sk next 2 dc, dc in next dc] twice, dc in

Continued on page 95

Shells Filet

Design by Peggy Longshore

SKILL LEVEL

 INTERMEDIATE

FINISHED SIZE

53½ x 80½ inches

MATERIALS

- Red Heart Super Saver medium (worsted) weight yarn **4 MEDIUM**
  (Solids: 7 oz/364 yds/198g per skein;
  Multis: 5 oz/244 yds/141g per skein):
      8 skeins #381 light blue
      1 skein #995 ocean
- Size G/6/4mm crochet hook or
  size needed to obtain gauge
- Tapestry needle

GAUGE

7 dc = 2 inches; 8 dc rows = 4 inches

PATTERN NOTES

Weave in ends as work progresses.

Join with a slip stitch unless otherwise stated.

Chain-3 at beginning of double crochet rows counts as first double crochet unless otherwise stated.

SPECIAL STITCHES

Block: Dc in each of next 3 indicated sts.
Mesh: Ch 1, sk next indicated st or ch, dc in next st.

INSTRUCTIONS

CENTER

Row 1 (RS): With light blue, ch 189, dc in 4th ch from hook *(beg 3 sk chs count as first dc)*, dc in each rem ch across, turn. *(187 dc)*

Row 2: Ch 3 *(see Pattern Notes)*, dc in each dc across, turn.

Row 3: Rep row 2.

Row 4: Ch 3, 2 **blocks** *(see Special Stitches)*, *mesh *(see Special Stitches)* 27 times, 2 blocks, rep from * twice, turn.

Rows 5–150: Work according to charts on pages 82 and 83. At end of last row, fasten off.

BORDER

Rnd 1: Hold piece with RS facing, join ocean with sc in sp formed by edge dc of last row, *ch 1, sc in sp formed by edge dc of next row, rep from * to next corner, ch 3, working across next side in unused lps of beg ch, sc in first lp, **ch 1, sk next lp, sc in next lp, rep from ** to corner, ch 3, working across next side, sc in sp formed by edge dc of first row, ***ch 1, sc in sp formed by edge dc of next row, rep from *** to next corner, ch 3, working across next side, sc in first dc, ****ch 1, sk next dc, sc in next dc, rep from **** to last corner, ch 3, join in beg sc.

Rnd 2: Sl st in next ch-1 sp, ch 1, sc in same sp, *ch 1, sk next sc, sc in next ch-1 sp, rep from * across to next corner ch-3 sp, (sc, ch 2, sc) in corner ch-3 sp, **ch 1, sk next sc, sc in next ch-1 sp, rep from ** across to next corner ch-3 sp, (sc, ch 2, sc) in corner ch-3 sp, ***ch 1, sk next sc, sc in next ch-1 sp, rep

from *** across to next corner ch-3 sp, (sc, ch 2, sc) in corner ch-3 sp, ****ch 1, sk next sc, sc in next ch-1 sp, rep from **** across to next corner ch-3 sp, (sc, ch 2, sc) in corner ch-3 sp, ch 1, join in beg sc. Fasten off.

TRIM

Note: Trim is worked in ch-1 sps, forming mesh bordering blocks around individual shells and around word "Shells." Work 2 Trims around individual shells and 1 around word.

Hold piece with RS facing, join ocean with sc around **post** *(see Stitch Guide)* of any corner dc, *ch 1, dc around post of next dc or in each ch-1 sp, rep from * around and work ch-2 in each corner, join in beg sc. Fasten off. ■

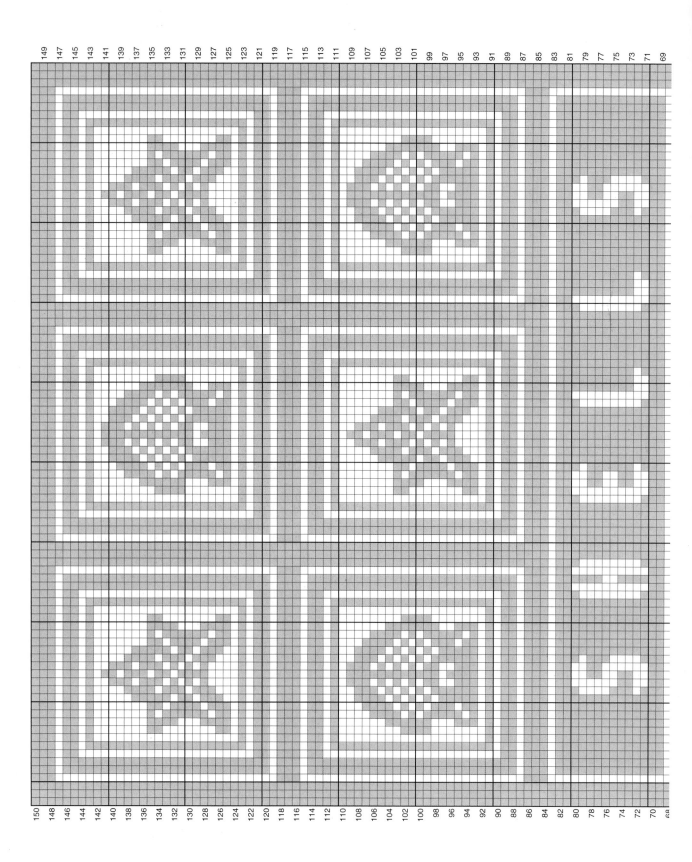

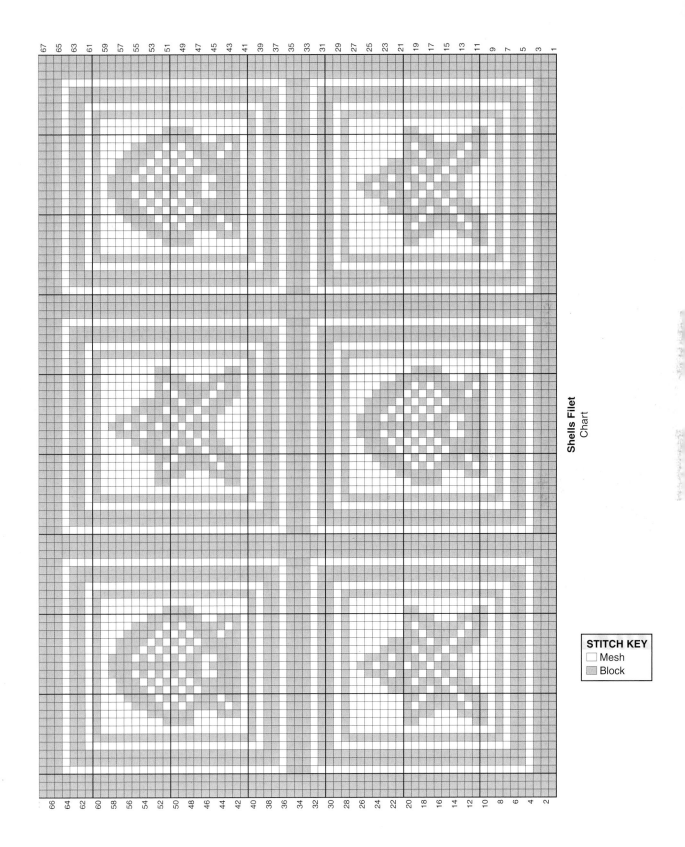

Shells Filet
Chart

STITCH KEY
☐ Mesh
▨ Block

Delicate Pineapples

Design by Judy Teague Treece

SKILL LEVEL

 EASY

FINISHED SIZE

48 x 64 inches

MATERIALS

- Red Heart Super Saver medium (worsted) weight yarn (7 oz/ 364 yds/198g per skein): 5 skeins #579 pale plum
- Size H/8/5mm crochet hook or size needed to obtain gauge
- Tapestry needle

GAUGE

Rnds 1 & 2 = 3½ inches
Block = 15 inches

PATTERN NOTES

Weave in ends as work progresses.

Join with a slip stitch unless otherwise stated.

Chain-3 at beginning of double crochet rounds counts as first double crochet unless otherwise stated.

Chain-5 at beginning of double crochet rounds counts as first double crochet and chain-2 space unless otherwise stated.

Chain-6 at beginning of double crochet rows counts as first double crochet and chain-3 space unless otherwise stated.

INSTRUCTIONS

BLOCK

Make 12.

Rnd 1 (RS): Ch 6, join in first ch to form ring, **ch 5** *(see Pattern Notes)*, dc in ring, [dc in ring, ch 2] 7 times, join in 3rd ch of beg ch-5. *(8 dc, 8 ch–2 sps)*

Rnd 2: Sl st in next ch-2 sp, **ch 3** *(see Pattern Notes)*, (dc, ch 2, 2 dc) in same sp, (2 dc, ch 2, 2 dc) in each rem ch-2, join in 3rd ch of beg ch-3. *(32 dc, 8 ch–2 sps)*

Rnd 3: Sl st in next st and in next ch-2 sp, ch 3, (dc, ch 2, 2 dc) in same ch, ch 4, *sc in next ch-2 sp, ch 4, (2 dc, ch 2, 2 dc) in next ch-2 sp, ch 4, rep from * twice, sc in next ch-2 sp, ch 4, join in 3rd ch of beg ch-3. *(16 dc, 4 sc, 8 ch–4 sps, 4 ch–2 sps)*

Rnd 4: Sl st in next st and in next ch-2 sp, ch 5, sc in same sp, *ch 6, (dc, ch 2, dc) in next sc, ch 6, (sc, ch 5, sc) in next ch-2 sp, rep from * twice, ch 6, (dc, ch 2, dc) in next sc, ch 6, join in 2nd sl st.

Rnd 5: Sl st in next ch-5 sp, ch 3, 6 dc in same sp *(beg base of pineapple)*, *ch 6, (dc, ch 1) twice in next ch-2 sp, dc in same sp, ch 6 **, 7 dc in next ch-5 sp *(base of pineapple)*, rep from * 3 times, ending last rep at **, join in 3rd ch of beg ch-3.

Rnd 6: Ch 1, sc in same ch as joining, *[ch 2, sc in next dc] 6 times, ch 6, sk next ch-6 sp, (dc, ch 1, dc) in each of next 2 ch-1 sps, ch 6, sk next ch-6 sp **, sc in next dc, rep from * 3 times, ending last rep at **, join in beg sc.

Continued on page 96

Rose Diamond

Design by Christine Moody

SKILL LEVEL
 EASY

FINISHED SIZE
33½ x 57 inches

MATERIALS
- Lion Brand Vanna's Choice medium (worsted) weight yarn (3½ oz/170 yds/100g per skein): 4 skeins #140 dusty rose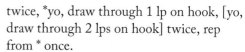
- Size I/9/5.5mm crochet hook or size needed to obtain gauge
- Tapestry needle

GAUGE
3 dc = 1 inch

PATTERN NOTES
Weave in ends as work progresses.

Afghan is worked lengthwise.

SPECIAL STITCHES
Mesh: Ch 2, sk next 2 indicated sts or chs, dc in next st.
Block: Dc in each of next 3 indicated sts, or dc in each of next 2 indicated chs, dc in next st.
Beginning increase block (beg inc block): Ch 5, dc in 4th ch from hook, dc in last ch, dc in next st.
Ending increase block (ending inc block): Yo, insert hook in indicated st, yo, draw lp through, yo, draw through 1 lp on hook, [yo, draw through 2 lps on hook] twice, *yo, draw through 1 lp on hook, [yo, draw through 2 lps on hook] twice, rep from * once.
Ending decrease block (ending dec block): Block leaving rem sts unworked.

INSTRUCTIONS

CENTER
Row 1: Ch 174, dc in 4th ch from hook *(first 3 chs count as first dc)*, dc in each rem ch across, turn. *(172 dc)*
Row 2: Beg inc block *(see Special Stitches)*, 2 **blocks** *(see Special Stitches)*, [2 **mesh** *(see Special Stitches)*, block, 2 mesh, 3 blocks] 6 times, 2 mesh, block, 2 mesh, 2 blocks, **ending inc block** *(see Special Stitches)*, turn.
Row 3: Beg inc block, block, [mesh, 2 blocks, 3 mesh, 2 blocks] 7 times, mesh, block, end inc block, turn.
Row 4: Beg inc block, block, [3 mesh, 2 blocks, mesh, 2 blocks] 7 times, 3 mesh, block, end inc block, turn.
Row 5: Beg inc block, block, 5 mesh, [3 blocks, 5 mesh] 7 times, block, end inc block, turn.
Row 6: Sl st in first 4 sts, beg block, block, [3 mesh, 2 blocks, mesh, 2 blocks] 7 times, 3 mesh, block, **ending dec block** *(see Special Stitches)*, turn.
Row 7: Sl st in first 4 sts, beg block, block, mesh, 2 blocks, [3 mesh, 2 blocks, mesh, 2 blocks] 6 times, 3 mesh, 2 blocks, mesh, block, end dec block, turn.

Continued on page 97

Black Pineapples

Design by Joyce Nordstrom

SKILL LEVEL

 INTERMEDIATE

FINISHED SIZE

51 x 78 inches

MATERIALS

- Red Heart Soft Yarn medium (worsted) weight yarn (5 oz/ 256 yds/140g per skein): 10 skeins #4614 black
- Size I/9/5.5mm crochet hook or size needed to obtain gauge
- Tapestry needle

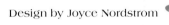

GAUGE

4 dc = 1 inch; 6 rows = 4 inches

PATTERN NOTES

Weave in ends as work progresses.

Chain-3 at beginning of double crochet rows counts as first double crochet unless otherwise stated.

Chain-10 at beginning of double treble crochet rows counts as first double treble crochet and chain-5 space unless otherwise stated.

SPECIAL STITCHES

Shell: (2 dc, ch 2, 2 dc) in indicated sp.
Picot: Ch 3, sl st in 3rd ch from hook.

INSTRUCTIONS

CENTER

Row 1 (RS): Ch 172, dc in 4th ch from hook *(beg 3 sk chs count as a dc)*, *ch 3, sk next 3 chs, dc in each of next 4 chs, ch 3, sk next 2 chs, sc in next ch, ch 3, sk next 2 chs, dc in each of next 4 chs, ch 3, sk next 3 chs, dc in each of next 2 chs, rep from * 7 times, turn.

Row 2: Ch 3 *(see Pattern Notes)*, *2 dc in next dc, ch 3, sk next ch-3 sp, **dc dec** *(see Stitch Guide)* in next 2 dc, dc in next dc, 2 dc in next dc, ch 4, sk next ch-3 sp, sc in next sc, ch 4, sk next ch-3 sp, 2 dc in next dc, dc in next dc, dc dec in next 2 dc, ch 3, sk next ch-3 sp, 2 dc in next dc, rep from * 7 times, dc in last dc, turn.

Row 3: Ch 3, *dc in next dc, 2 dc in next dc, ch 3, sk next ch-3 sp, dc dec in next 2 dc, dc in next dc, 2 dc in next dc, ch 4, sk next ch-4 sp, sc in next sc, ch 4, sk next ch-4 sp, 2 dc in next dc, dc in next dc, dc dec in next 2 dc, ch 3, sk next ch-3 sp, 2 dc in next dc, dc in next dc, rep from * 7 times, dc in last dc, turn.

Row 4: Ch 3, *dc in each of next 2 dc, 2 in next dc, ch 3, sk next ch-3 sp, dc dec in next 2 dc, dc in next dc, 2 dc in next dc, sk next ch-4 sp, sk next sc, sk next ch-4 sp, 2 dc in next dc, dc in next dc, dc dec in next 2 dc, ch 3, sk next ch-3 sp, 2 in next dc, dc in each of next 2 dc, rep from * 7 times, dc in last dc, turn.

Row 5: Ch 10 *(see Pattern Notes)*, *dc dec in next 2 dc, dc in next dc, 2 dc in next dc, ch 3, sk next ch-3 sp, dc dec in next 2 dc, dc in each of next 4 dc, dc dec in next 2 dc, ch 3, sk next ch-3 sp, 2 dc in next dc, dc in next dc, dc dec in next 2 dc **, ch 11, rep from * across, ending last rep at **, ch 5, dtr in last dc, turn.

Row 6: Ch 1, sc in first dtr, ch 4, sk next ch-5 sp, *dc dec in next 2 dc, dc in next dc, 2 dc in next dc, ch 3, sk next ch-3 sp, dc dec in next 2 dc, dc in each of next 2 dc, dc dec in next 2 dc, ch 3, sk next ch-3 sp, 2 dc in next dc, dc in next dc, dc dec in next 2 dc, ch 4 **, sc in 6th ch of next ch-11 sp, ch 4, rep from * across, ending last rep at **, sc in 6th ch of beg ch-10, turn.

Row 7: Ch 1, sc in first sc, *ch 3, sk next ch-4 sp, dc dec in next 2 dc, dc in next dc, 2 dc in next dc, ch 3, sk next ch-3 sp, [dc dec in next 2 dc] twice, ch 3, sk next ch-3 sp, 2 dc in next dc, dc in next dc, dc dec in next 2 dc, ch 3, sk next ch-4 sp, sc in next sc, rep from * across, turn.

Row 8: Ch 1, sc in first sc, *ch 3, sk next ch-3 sp, dc in each of next 4 dc, ch 3, sk next ch-3 sp, dc in each of next 2 dc, ch 3, sk next ch-3 sp, dc in each of next 4 dc, ch 3, sk next ch-3 sp, sc in next sc, rep from * across, turn.

Row 9: Ch 1, sc in first sc, *ch 4, sk next ch-3 sp, 2 dc in next dc, dc in next dc, dc dec in next 2 dc, ch 3, sk next ch-3 sp, 2 dc in each of next 2 dc, ch 3, sk next ch-3 sp, dc dec in next 2 dc, dc in next dc, 2 dc in next dc, ch 4, sk next ch-3 sp, sc in next sc, rep from * across, turn.

Row 10: Ch 1, sc in first sc, *ch 4, sk next ch-4 sp, 2 dc in next dc, dc in next dc, dc dec in next 2 dc, ch 3, sk next ch-3 sp, 2 dc in next dc, dc in each of next 2 dc, 2 dc in next dc, ch 3, sk next ch-3 sp, dc dec in next 2 dc, dc in next dc, 2 dc in next dc, ch 4, sk next ch-4 sp, sc in next sc, rep from * across, turn.

Row 11: Ch 5, sk next ch-4 sp, *2 dc in next dc, dc in next dc, dc dec in next 2 dc, ch 3, sk next ch-3 sp, 2 dc in next dc, dc in each of next 4 dc, 2 dc in next dc, ch 3, sk next ch-3 sp, dc dec in next 2 dc, dc in next dc, 2 dc in next dc **, sk next 2 ch-4 sps, rep from * across, ending last rep at **, sk next ch-4 sp, dtr in next sc, turn.

Row 12: Ch 3, dc in each of next 2 dc, dc dec in next 2 dc, *ch 3, sk next ch-3 sp, 2 dc in next dc, dc in next dc, dc dec in next 2 dc, ch 11, dc dec in next 2 dc, dc in next dc, 2 dc in next dc, ch 3, sk next ch-3 sp, dc dec in next 2 dc **, dc in each of next 4 dc, dc dec in next 2 dc, rep from * across, ending last rep at **, dc in each of next 2 dc, dc in 5th ch of beg ch-5, turn.

Row 13: Ch 3, dc in next dc, dc dec in next 2 dc, *ch 3, sk next ch-3 sp, 2 dc in next dc, dc in next dc, dc dec in next 2 dc, ch 4, sc in 6th ch of next ch-11 sp, ch 4, dc dec in next 2 dc, dc in next dc, 2 in next dc, ch 3, sk next ch-3 sp, dc dec in next 2 dc **, dc in each of next 2 dc, dc dec in next 2 dc, rep from * across, ending last rep at **, dc in next dc, dc in 3rd ch of beg ch-3, turn.

Row 14: Ch 3, *dc dec in next 2 dc, ch 3, sk next ch-3 sp, 2 dc in next dc, dc in next dc, dc dec in next 2 dc, ch 3, sc in next sc, ch 3, dc dec in next 2 dc, dc in next dc, 2 dc in next dc, ch 3, sk next ch-3 sp, dc dec in next 2 dc, rep from * across, dc in 3rd ch of beg ch-3.

Row 15: Ch 3, dc in next dc, *ch 3, sk next ch-3 sp, dc in each of next 4 dc, ch 3, sk next ch-3 sp, sc in next sc, ch 3, sk next ch-3 sp, dc in each of next 4 dc, ch 3, sk next ch-3 sp **, dc in each of next 2 dc, rep from * 7 times, ending last rep at **, dc in next dc, dc in 3rd ch of beg ch-3, turn.

Rows 16–99: [Rep rows 2–15 consecutively] 6 times. At end of last row, fasten off.

BORDERS
Top Border
First Pineapple

Row 1: Hold piece with RS facing and last row worked at top, join yarn in first st in right-hand corner, ch 3, **shell** *(see Special Stitches)* in next ch-3 sp, ch 4, sk next 4 dc, sc in next ch-3 sp, ch 6, sk next sc, sc in next ch-3 sp, ch 4, sk next 4 dc, shell in next ch-3 sp, dc in dc, turn.

Row 2: Ch 3, shell in ch-2 sp of next shell, ch 1, 9 dc in ch-6 sp, ch 1, shell in ch-2 sp of next shell, dc in 3rd ch of beg ch-3, turn.

Row 3: Ch 3, shell in ch-2 sp of next shell,

ch 1, sc in next dc, [ch 3, sk next dc, sc in next dc] 4 times, ch 1, shell in ch-2 sp of next shell, dc in 3rd ch of beg ch-3, turn.

Row 4: Ch 3, shell in ch-2 sp of next shell, ch 1, sc in next ch-3 sp, [ch 3, sc in next ch-3 sp] 3 times, ch 1, shell in ch-2 sp of next shell, dc in 3rd ch of beg ch-3, turn.

Row 5: Ch 3, shell in ch-2 sp of next shell, ch 1, sc in next ch-3 sp, [ch 3, sc in next ch-3 sp] twice, ch 1, shell in ch-2 sp of next shell, dc in 3rd ch of beg ch-3, turn.

Row 6: Ch 3, shell in ch-2 sp of next shell, ch 1, sc in next ch-3 sp, ch 3, sc in next ch-3 sp, ch 1, shell in ch-2 sp of next shell, dc in 3rd ch of beg ch-3, turn.

Row 7: Ch 3, shell in ch-2 sp of next shell, ch 1, sc in next ch-3 sp, ch 1, shell in ch-2 sp of next shell, dc in 3rd ch of beg ch-3, turn.

Row 8: Ch 3, shell in ch-2 sp of next shell, sk next sc, shell in ch-2 sp of next shell, dc in 3rd ch of beg ch-3, turn.

Row 9: Ch 3, 2 dc in ch-2 sp of each of next 2 shells, dc in 3rd ch of beg ch-3. Fasten off.

2nd Pineapple

Row 1: Join yarn in next dc on last row from First Pineapple, ch 3, shell in next ch-3 sp, ch 4, sk next 4 dc, sc in next ch-3 sp, ch 6, sk next sc, sc in next ch-3 sp, ch 4, sk next
4 dc, shell in next ch-3 sp, dc in dc, turn.

Rows 2–9: Rep rows 2–9 of First Pineapple.

3rd Pineapple

Row 1: Join yarn in next dc on last row from last completed pineapple, ch 3, shell in next ch-3 sp, ch 4, sk next 4 dc, sc in next ch-3 sp, ch 6, sk next sc, sc in next ch-3 sp, ch 4, sk next 4 dc, shell in next ch-3 sp, dc in dc, turn.

Rows 2–9: Rep rows 2–9 of First Pineapple.

4th–7th Pineapples

Work same as 3rd Pineapple.

Bottom Border
First Pineapple

Row 1: Hold piece with RS facing and beg ch at top, join yarn in unused lp of first ch in right-hand corner, ch 3, shell in next ch-3 sp, ch 4, sk unused lp at base of each of next 4 dc, sc in next ch-3 sp, ch 6, sk unused lp at base of next sc, sc in next ch-3 sp, ch 4, sk unused lp at base of each of next 4 dc, shell in next ch-3 sp, dc in unused lp at base of next dc, turn.

Rows 2–9: Rep rows 2–9 of First Pineapple.

2nd Pineapple

Row 1: Join yarn in next unused lp on beg ch from First Pineapple, ch 3, shell in next ch-3 sp, ch 4, sk unused lp at base of each of next 4 dc, sc in next ch-3 sp, ch 6, sk unused lp at base of next sc, sc in next ch-3 sp, ch 4, sk unused lp at base of each of next 4 dc, shell in next ch-3 sp, dc in unused lp at base of next dc, turn.

Rows 2–9: Rep rows 2–9 of First Pineapple.

3rd Pineapple

Row 1: Join yarn in next unused lp on beg ch from last completed pineapple, ch 3, shell in next ch-3 sp, ch 4, sk unused lp at base of each of next 4 dc, sc in next ch-3 sp, ch 6, sk unused lp at base of next sc, sc in next ch-3 sp, ch 4, sk unused lp at base of each of next 4 dc, shell in next ch-3 sp, dc in unused lp at base of next dc, turn.

Rows 2–9: Rep rows 2–9 of First Pineapple.

4th–7th Pineapples

Work same as 3rd Pineapple.

EDGING

Hold piece with RS facing, join yarn in sp formed by any edge dc or ch-3, ch 1, (sc, **picot** *(see Special Stitches)*, sc) in same sp, working around entire afghan, (sc, picot, sc) in sp formed by each rem edge dc or ch-3 and (sc, picot) in each edge sc, join in beg sc. Fasten off. ∎

Double Happiness

Design by Maria Merlino

SKILL LEVEL
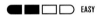 EASY

FINISHED SIZE
55 x 76 inches

MATERIALS
- Red Heart Super Saver medium (worsted) weight yarn (7 oz/ 364 yds/198g per skein): 5 skeins #319 cherry red
- Sizes I/9/5.5mm and K/10½/6.5mm crochet hooks or size needed to obtain gauge
- Tapestry needle

GAUGE
With size I hook: 5 extended dc = 1¾ inches; 3 rows = 2 inches

PATTERN NOTES
Weave in ends as work progresses.

Join with a slip stitch unless otherwise stated.

Chain-3 at beginning of extended double crochet rows counts as first extended double crochet unless otherwise stated.

SPECIAL STITCHES
Extended double crochet (extended dc): Yo, insert hook in indicated st, yo, draw lp through, yo, draw through 1 lp on hook, [yo, draw through 2 lps on hook] twice.

Mesh: Ch 2, sk next 2 indicated sts or chs, extended dc in next st.

Block: Extended dc in each of next 3 indicated sts, or 2 extended dc in indicated ch sp, extended dc in next st.

INSTRUCTIONS

CENTER
Row 1 (RS): With size K hook, ch 183, change to size I hook, **extended dc** *(see Special Stitches)* in 4th ch from hook *(beg 3 sk chs count as a extended dc)*, extended dc in each rem ch across, turn. *(181 extended dc)*

Row 2: Ch 3 *(see Pattern Notes)*, **block** *(see Special Stitches)*, **mesh** *(see Special Stitches)* 58 times, block, turn.

Row 3: Block, 58 mesh, block, turn.

Row 4: Block, 5 mesh, block, 17 mesh, block, 34 mesh, block, turn.

Rows 5–100: Work according to chart on page 94. At end of last row, ch 1, turn.

BORDER
2 sc in first st, working across next side, 2 sc in end of each of next 100 rows, working across next side in unused lps of beg ch, 3 sc in first lp, sc in each lp across to last lp, 3 sc in last lp, working across next side, 2 sc in end of each of next 100 rows, working across next side, 3 sc in first dc, sc in each dc across to beg sc, sc in same dc as beg 2 sc, join in beg sc. Fasten off. *(770 sc)* ■

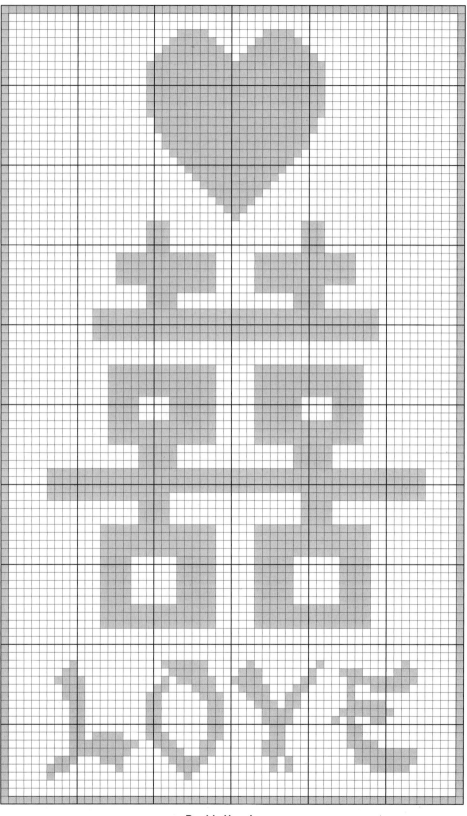

STITCH KEY
☐ Mesh
▨ Block

Double Happiness
Chart

PINEAPPLE CONNECTION
Continued from page 76

sk next ch-3 sp, [sc in next ch-3 sp, ch 3] twice, sc in next ch-3 sp, ch 4, sk next ch-3 sp, shell in ch-1 sp of next shell, ch 1, sk next ch-1 sp, dc in each of next 10 dc, rep from * twice, turn. *(6 shells, 40 dc, 18 sc, 6 ch-4 sps, 6 ch-3 sps, 6 ch-1 sps)*

Row 8: Ch 2, dc in each of first 10 dc, *ch 1, shell in ch-1 sp of next shell, ch 5, sk next ch-4 sp, sc in next ch-3 sp, ch 3, sc in next ch-3 sp, ch 5, sk next ch-3 sp, shell in ch-1 sp of next shell, ch 1, sk next ch-1 sp, dc in each of next 10 dc, rep from * twice, turn. *(6 shells, 40 dc, 18 sc, 6 ch-5 sps, 3 ch-3 sps, 6 ch-1 sps)*

Row 9: Ch 2, dc in each of first 10 dc, *ch 1, shell in ch-1 sp of next shell, ch 2, sk next ch-5 sp, 7 dc in next ch-3 sp *(base of pineapple)*, ch 2, sk next ch-5 sp, shell in ch-1 sp of next shell, sk next ch-1 sp, dc in each of next 10 dc, rep from * twice, turn. *(6 shells, 40 dc, 6 ch-2 sps, 3 ch-1 sps)*

Row 10: Ch 2, dc in each of first 10 dc, *ch 1, shell in ch-1 sp of next shell, ch 1, sk next ch-2 sp, [dc in next dc, ch 1] 7 times, sk next ch-2 sp, shell in ch-1 sp of next shell, ch 1, sk next ch-1 sp, dc in each of next 10 dc, rep from * twice, turn. *(6 shells, 61 dc, 30 ch-1 sps)*

Rows 11–80: [Rep rows 4–10 consecutively] 10 times.

Rows 81–85: Rep rows 4–8.

TOP BORDER

Row 1 (WS): Ch 1, sc in each of first 10 dc, *sk next ch-1 sp, sc in each of next 2 dc, sc in next ch-1 sp, sc in each of next 2 dc, 4 sc in next ch-5 sp, 2 sc in next ch-3 sp, 4 sc in next ch-5 sp, sc in each of next 2 dc, sc in next ch-1 sp, sc in each of next 2 dc, sk next ch-1 sp, sc in each of next 10 sc, rep from * twice, turn. *(100 sc)*

Row 2 (RS): Ch 1, sc in each of first 2 sc, ch 3, sk next sc, *sc in each of next 4 sc, [ch 3, sk next sc, sc in next sc] twice, ch 3, sk next sc, rep from * to last 7 sc, sc in each of next 4 sc, ch 3, sk next sc, sc in each of last 2 sc, turn.

Row 3: Ch 1, sc in first sc, ch 2, sc in next ch-3 sp, ch 5, sk next 4 sc, *[sc in next ch-3 sp, ch 3] twice, sc in next ch-3 sp, ch 5, sk next 4 sc, rep from * to last ch-3 sp, sc in last ch-3 sp, ch 2, sk next sc, sc in last sc, turn.

Row 4: Ch 1, sc in next ch-2 sp, (4 dc, ch 3, sl st in first ch, 4 dc) in next ch-5 sp, *sc in next ch-3 sp, ch 3, sc in next ch-3 sp, (4 dc, ch 3, sl st in first ch, 4 dc) in next ch-5 sp, rep from * across, sc in last ch-2 sp, sl st in last sc. Fasten off.

BOTTOM BORDER

Row 1 (WS): Hold Center with WS facing and beg ch at top, join yarn in unused lp of first ch of beg ch, ch 1, sc in same lp, working in rem unused lps of beg ch, sc in each of next 22 lps, 2 sc in next lp, [sc in each of next 23 lps, 2 sc in next lp] 3 times, turn. *(100 sc)*

Rows 2–4: Rep rows 2–4 of Top Border. ∎

HERITAGE FILET
Continued from page 79

each of next 6 dc, [2 dc in next ch-2 sp, dc in next dc] twice **, [ch 2, sk next ch-2 sp, dc in next dc] twice, rep from * 9 times, ending last rep at **, ch 2, sk next ch-2 sp, dc in last dc, change color to black in last dc, turn. Fasten off light coral.

Row 7: Ch 1, sc in first dc, 2 sc in each ch-2 sp and sc in each rem dc across, turn.

Row 8: Ch 1, sc in each sc across, turn.

Row 9: Ch 1,

sc in each sc across, change color to buff in last sc, turn. Fasten off black.

Row 10: Rep row 8.

Row 11: Ch 5, sk next 2 sc, dc in next sc, *ch 2, sk next 2 sc, dc in next sc, rep from * across, turn.

Row 12: Ch 5, sk next ch-2 sp, dc in next dc, *ch 2, sk next ch-2 sp, dc in next dc, rep from * across, turn.

Rows 13–15: Rep row 12.

Row 16: Ch 1, sc in first dc, 2 sc in each ch-2 sp and sc in each rem dc across, change color to black in last sc, turn. Fasten off buff.

Rows 17–19: Rep row 8. Change color to light coral in last sc of row 19. Fasten off black.

Rows 20–131: [Rep rows 4–19 consecutively] 7 times.

Rows 132–137: Rep rows 4–9. At end of last row, fasten off.

TRIM

Step 1: Hold piece with RS facing, join turqua between 2 sc at bottom of first ch-2 sp on row 11, **beg pc** *(see Special Stitches)* in same sp, sl st in ch-2 at top of sp, ch 3;

Step 2: *now working in 2nd ch-2 sp on next ascending row, **pc** *(see Special Stitches)* in ch-2 at bottom of sp, sl st in ch-2 at top of sp, ch 3, rep from * twice;

Step 3: now working in 2nd ch-2 sp on next ascending row, pc in ch-2 at bottom of sp, sl st between 2 sc of row 16 at top of sp, ch 3;

Step 4: now working in 2nd ch-2 sp on next descending row, pc in ch-2 at bottom of sp, sl st in ch-2 at top of sp, ch 3, rep from * 3 times;

Step 5: now working in 2nd ch-2 sp on next descending row, pc between 2 sc at bottom of sp, sl st over ch-2 at top of sp. Rep Steps 2–5 across section. Fasten off. Work Trim in same manner on 7 rem buff sections.

BORDERS

Top Border

Row 1 (RS): Hold piece with RS facing and row 1 to right, join black in end of row 1, ch 1, working in ends of rem rows, sc evenly spaced across, turn.

Row 2: Ch 1, sc in each sc across, turn.

Row 3: Ch 1, sc in each sc across. Fasten off.

Bottom Border

Row 1 (RS): Hold piece with RS facing and row 137 to right, join black in end of row 137, ch 1, working in ends of rem rows, sc evenly spaced across, turn.

Row 2: Ch 1, sc in each sc across, turn.

Row 3: Ch 1, sc in each sc across, turn.

Rnd 4: Now working in rnds, sl st in each st around entire afghan, working 2 sl sts in each corner, join in beg sl st. Fasten off. ■

DELICATE PINEAPPLES

Continued from page 85

Rnd 7: Sl st in next ch-2 sp, sc in same sp, *[ch 2, sc in next ch-2 sp] 5 times, ch 4, sk next ch-6 sp, [(dc, ch 1) twice, dc] in each of next 2 ch-1 sps, ch 4, sk next ch-6 sp **, sc in next ch-2 sp, rep from * 3 times, ending last rep at **, join in beg sc.

Rnd 8: Sl st in next ch-2 sp, sc in same sp, *[ch 2, sc in next ch-2 sp] 4 times, ch 5, sk next ch-4 sp, (dc, ch 1, dc) in each of next 4 ch-1 sps, ch 5, sk next ch-4 sp **, sc in next sc, rep from * 3 times, ending last rep at **, join in beg sc.

Rnd 9: Sl st in next ch-2 sp, sc in same sp, *[ch 2, sc in next ch-2 sp] 3 times, ch 5, sk next ch-5 sp, [(dc, ch 1) twice, dc] in each of next 4 ch-1 sps, ch 5, sk next ch-5 sp **, sc in next ch-2 sp, rep from * 3 times, ending last rep at **, join in beg sc.

Rnd 10: Sl st in next ch-2 sp, sc in same sp, *[ch 2, sc in next ch-2 sp] twice, ch 5, sk next ch-5 sp, (dc, ch 1, dc) in each of next

4 ch-1 sps, ch 4, (dc, ch 1, dc) in each of next 4 ch-1 sps, ch 5, sk next ch-5 sp **, sc in next ch-2 sp, rep from * 3 times, ending last rep at **, join in beg sc.

Rnd 11: Sl st in next ch-2 sp, sc in same sp, *ch 2, sc in next ch-2 sp, ch 5, (dc, ch 1, dc) in each of next 4 ch-1 sps, (3 dc, ch 2, 3 dc) in next ch-4 sp *(corner)*, (dc, ch 1, dc) in each of next 4 ch-1 sps, ch 5, sk next ch-5 sp **, sc in next ch-2 sp, rep from * 3 times, ending last rep at **, join in beg sc.

Rnd 12: Sl st in next ch-2 sp, sc in same sp, *ch 6, sk next ch-5 sp, (dc, ch 1, dc) in each of next 4 ch-1 sps, sk next dc, dc in each of next 3 dc, (2 dc, ch 2, 2 dc) in next corner ch-2 sp *(corner)*, sc in each of next 3 dc, (dc, ch 1, dc) in each of next 4 ch-1 sps, ch 6, sk next ch-5 sp **, sc in next ch-2 sp, rep from * 3 times, ending last rep at **, join in beg sc.

Rnd 13: Ch 1, sc in same sc, *6 sc in next ch-6 sp, sc in each dc and in each ch-1 sp

to next corner ch-2 sp, (2 sc, ch 2, 2 sc) in corner ch-2 sp *(corner)*, sc in each dc and in each ch-1 sp to next ch-6 sp, 6 sc in next ch-6 sp **, sc in next sc, rep from * 3 times, ending last rep at **, join in beg sc.

Rnd 14: Ch 3, *dc in each sc to corner ch-2 sp **, (2 dc, ch 2, 2 dc) in corner ch-2 sp *(corner)*, rep from * 3 times, ending last rep at **, join in 3rd ch of beg ch-3. Fasten off.

ASSEMBLY

Working in **back lps** *(see Stitch Guide)* only, sew Blocks tog in 4 rows of 3 Blocks each.

EDGING

Hold piece with RS facing, join yarn in any dc, ch 3, (2 dc, ch 3, sc in first ch, 3 dc) in same dc, *ch 3, sk next 5 sts, sc in next st, ch 3, sk next 5 sts, (3 dc, ch 3, sc in first ch, 3 dc) in next st, sk next 5 sts, rep from * around, join in 3rd ch of beg ch-3. Fasten off. ∎

ROSE DIAMOND
Continued from page 86

Row 8: Sl st in first 4 sts, beg block, 2 blocks, [2 mesh, block, 2 mesh, 3 blocks] 6 times, 2 mesh, block, 2 mesh, 2 blocks, end dec block, turn.

Row 9: Sl st in first 4 sts, beg block, [2 mesh, 3 blocks, 2 mesh, block] 6 times, 2 mesh, 3 blocks, 2 mesh, end dec block, turn.
Note: Using Special Stitches, work the following rows according to chart.
Rows 10–49: [Rep rows 2–9 consecutively] 5 times.
Rows 50–56: Rep rows 2–8.

Row 57: Sl st in each of first 4 sts, ch 3, dc in each st and in each ch across to last 3 sts, leaving last 3 sts unworked. Fasten off. ∎

STITCH KEY
- ☐ Mesh
- ▨ Block
- ☒ Beg Block
- ◉ Beg Inc Block
- ◆ End Inc Block
- ◈ End Dec Block

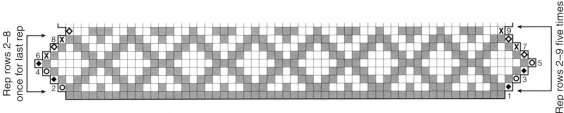

Rose Diamond
Chart

Generations of Baby

Generations of
babies can be
wrapped in these
beautiful heirloom
afghans. Stitch
a blankie that
is sure to be a
lasting treasure.

Ring Around the Rosie Baby Afghan

Design by Renee' Barnes

SKILL LEVEL

■■■□ INTERMEDIATE

FINISHED SIZE

42 inches in diameter

MATERIALS

- Bernat Softee Baby light (light worsted) weight yarn (5 oz/ 468 yds/140g per ball):
    2 balls each #02001 pink and #02000 white
    1 ball #02004 mint
- Size F/5/3.75mm crochet hook or size needed to obtain gauge
- Tapestry needle

GAUGE

Hexagon = 6 inches from flat side to flat side; 6¾ inches in diameter

PATTERN NOTES

Weave in ends as work progresses.

Join with a slip stitch unless otherwise stated.

Chain-3 at beginning of double crochet rounds count as first double crochet unless otherwise stated.

INSTRUCTIONS

ROSE HEXAGON

Make 13.
Rnd 1 (RS): With pink, ch 4, join with in first ch to form a ring, **ch 3** *(see Pattern Notes)*, 11 dc in ring, join in 3rd ch of beg ch-3. *(12 dc)*

Rnd 2: Ch 1, 5 dc in next dc *(petal)*, *sl st in next dc, 5 dc in next dc *(petal)*, rep from * 4 times, join in joining sl st. *(6 petals, 6 sl sts)*

Rnd 3: Ch 3, working behind dc of previous rnd, *sl st in next sl st, ch 3, rep from * 4 times, join in joining sl st. *(6 sl sts, 6 ch-3 sps)*

Rnd 4: Working behind petals, sl st in next ch-3 sp, 7 tr in same sp *(petal)*, sl st in next sl st, *7 tr in next ch-3 sp *(petal)*, sl st in next sl st, rep from * 4 times, join in joining sl st. Fasten off. *(6 petals, 6 sl sts)*

Rnd 5: Join mint in 4th tr of any petal, ch 7, *sl st in 4th tr of next petal, ch 7, rep from * 5 times, join in joining sl st. *(6 sl sts, 6 ch-7 sps)*

Rnd 6: Sl st in next ch-7 sp, ch 3, 9 dc in same sp, 10 dc in each rem ch-7 sp, join in 3rd ch of beg ch-3. Fasten off. *(60 dc)*

Rnd 7: Join white in sp between last dc and beg ch-3 of previous rnd, ch 3, (dc, ch 2, 2 dc) in same sp, *dc in next dc, hdc in next dc, sc in each of next 6 dc, hdc in next dc, dc in next dc, (2 dc, ch 2, 2 dc) in sp between last dc and next dc, rep from * 4 times, dc in next dc, hdc in next dc, sc in each of next 6 dc, hdc in next dc, dc in next dc, join in 3rd ch of beg ch-3. *(36 dc, 12 hdc, 36 sc, 6 ch-2 sps)*

Rnd 8: Sl st in next dc, sl st in ch-2 sp, ch 3, (dc, ch 2, 2 dc) in same sp,* sk next dc, dc in each of next 12 sts, sk next dc, (2 dc, ch 2, 2 dc) in next ch-2 sp, rep from * 4 times, sk next dc, dc in each of next 12 sts, sk next dc, join in 3rd ch of beg ch-3. Fasten off. *(96 dc, 6 ch-2 sps)*

Continued on page 116

Pink Flowers Crib Cover

Design by Lisa Pflug

SKILL LEVEL
 INTERMEDIATE

FINISHED SIZE
32 x 37 inches

MATERIALS
- Bernat Softee Baby light (light worsted) weight yarn (5 oz/ 468 yds/140g per ball):
  3 balls #02001 pink
  2 balls #02000 white
- Size G/6/4.00mm crochet hook or size needed to obtain gauge
- Tapestry needle

GAUGE
17 sc = 4 inches; 10 sc rows = 2 inches

PATTERN NOTES
Weave in ends as work progresses.

Join with a slip stitch unless otherwise stated.

Chain-3 at beginning of double crochet rows count as first double crochet unless otherwise stated.

Chain-6 at beginning of double crochet rounds count as first treble crochet and chain-2 space unless otherwise stated.

SPECIAL STITCHES
Cluster (cl): Holding back last lp of each dc on hook, 3 dc in sp indicated, yo and draw through all 4 lps on hook.

Treble crochet cluster (tr cl): Holding back last lp of each tr on hook, tr in each of next 3 indicated sts, yo and draw through all 4 lps on hook.
Picot: Ch 3, sl st in first ch.

INSTRUCTIONS

PANEL A
Make 2.
Row 1 (WS): With pink, ch 42, sc in 2nd ch from hook, sc in each rem ch across, turn. *(41 sc)*
Row 2 (RS): Ch 1, sc in each sc across, turn.
Rows 3–8: Rep row 2.
Row 9: Ch 1, sc in each of first 9 sc, ch 1, sk next sc, sc in each of next 21 sc, ch 1, sk next sc, sc in last 9 sc, turn. *(39 sc, 2 ch-1 sps)*
Row 10: Ch 1, sc in each of first 9 sc, (sc, ch 7, sc, ch 9, sc, ch 7, sc) in next ch-1 sp *(flower base)*, sc in each of next 21 sc, (sc, ch 7, sc, ch 9, sc, ch 7, sc) in next ch-1 sp, sc in each of last 9 sc, turn. *(2 flower bases, 39 sc)*
Row 11: Ch 1, sc in each of first 9 sc, keeping ch sps to back of work, sc in ch-1 sp on 2nd row below between 2nd and 3rd sc of next flower base, sk 4th sc of flower base, sc in each of next 21 sc on previous, sc in ch-1 sp on 2nd row below between 2nd and 3rd sc of next flower base, sk 4th sc of flower base, sc in each of last 9 sc on previous, turn.
Row 12: Ch 1, sc in each of next 6 sc, insert hook in next ch-7 sp of flower base, sc in next sc on previous row, sc in each of next 5 sc, insert hook in next ch-7 sp of same flower base, sc in next sc on previous row, sc in each of next 15 sc, insert hook in next ch-7 sp of

flower base, sc in next sc on previous row, sc in each of next 5 sc, insert hook in next ch-7 sp of same flower base, sc in next sc on previous row, sc in each of last 6 sc, turn. *(41 sc)*

Row 13: Rep row 2.

Row 14: Ch 1, sc in each of first 7 sc, 5 dc in ch-9 lp of next flower base, sk next 5 sc on previous row behind 5 dc just made, sc in each of next 17 sc, 5 dc in ch-9 lp of next flower base, sk next 5 sc on previous row behind 5 dc just made, sc in each of last 7 sc, turn.

Row 15: Ch 1, sc in each of first 7 sc, working behind next 5 dc, sc in each of next 5 sk sc on 2nd row below, sc in each of next 17 sc on previous row, working behind next 5 dc, sc in each of next 5 sk sc on 2nd row below, sc in each of last 7 sc, turn. *(41 sc)*

Rows 16–24: Rep row 2.

Row 25: Ch 1, sc in each of first 20 sc, ch 1, sk next sc, sc in each of last 20 sc, turn. *(40 sc, 1 ch-1 sp)*

Row 26: Ch 1, sc in each of first 20 sc, (sc, ch 7, sc, ch 9, sc, ch 7, sc) in next ch-1 sp *(flower base)*, sc in each of last 20 sc, turn. *(1 flower base, 40 sc)*

Row 27: Ch 1, sc in each of first 20 sc, keeping ch sps to back of work, sc in ch-1 sp on 2nd row below between 2nd and 3rd sc of next flower base, sk 4th sc of flower base, sc in each of last 20 sc, turn. *(41 sc)*

Row 28: Ch 1, sc in each of first 17 sc, insert hook in next ch-7 sp of flower base, sc in next sc on previous row, sc in each of next 5 sc, insert hook in next ch-7 sp of same flower base, sc in next sc on previous row, sc in each of last 17 sc, turn.

Row 29: Rep row 2.

Row 30: Ch 1, sc in each of first 18 sc, 5 dc in ch-9 lp of next flower base, sk next 5 sc on previous row behind 5 dc just made, sc in each of last 18 sc, turn.

Row 31: Ch 1, sc in each of first 18 sc, working behind next 5 dc, sc in each of next 5 sk sc on 2nd row below, sc in each of last 18 sc, turn.

Rows 32–42: Rep row 2.

Rows 43–49: Rep rows 9–15.

Rows 50–57: Rep row 2. At end of last row, fasten off.

Row 58: Hold piece with RS facing, join white in first sc, ch 1, sc in same sc, [ch 1, sk next sc, sc in next sc] 20 times, turn. *(21 sc, 20 ch-1 sps)*

Row 59: Ch 3 *(see Pattern Notes)*, [cl *(see Special Stitches)* in next ch-1 sp, ch 1] 19 times, cl in next ch-1 sp, dc in last sc, turn. *(20 cl, 2 dc, 19 ch-1 sps)*

Row 60: Ch 1, sc in first dc, [ch 1, sk next cl, sc in next ch-1 sp] 19 times, ch 1, sk next cl, sc in 3rd ch of beg ch-3, turn. *(21 sc, 20 ch-1 sps)*

Row 61: Ch 3, [cl in next ch-1 sp, ch 1] 19 times, cl in next ch-1 sp, dc in last sc, turn. *(20 cl, 2 dc, 19 ch-1 sps)*

Rows 62–87: [Rep rows 60 and 61 alternately] 13 times.

Row 88: Rep row 60. At end of row, fasten off.

Row 89: Hold piece with RS facing, join pink in first sc, ch 1, sc in each sc and in each ch-1 sp across, turn. *(41 sc)*

Rows 90–145: Rep rows 2–57.

PANEL 2

Make 1.

Row 1 (RS): With white, ch 42, sc in 2nd ch from hook, *ch 1, sk next sc, sc in next sc, rep from * across, turn. *(41 sc)*

Row 2: Ch 3, [cl in next ch-1 sp, ch 1] 18 times, cl in next ch-1 sp, dc in last sc, turn. *(20 cl, 2 dc)*

Row 3: Ch 1, sc in first dc, [ch 1, sk cl, sc in next cl] 18 times, ch 1, sk next cl, sc in 3rd ch of beg ch-3, turn. *(41 sts)*

Rows 4–31: [Rep rows 2 and 3 alternately] 14 times. At end of last row, fasten off.

Row 32: Hold piece with WS facing, join pink in first sc, ch 1, sc in each sc and in each ch-1 sp across, turn. *(41 sc)*

Rows 33–86: Rep rows 2–56 of Panel 1. At end of last row, fasten off.

Row 87: Hold piece with RS facing, join white in first sc, ch 1, sc in same sc, [ch 1, sk next sc, sc in next sc] 20 times, turn. *(21 sc, 20 ch-1 sps)*

Row 88: Ch 3, [cl in next ch-1 sp, ch 1] 19 times, cl in next ch-1 sp, dc in last sc, turn. *(20 cl, 2 dc, 19 ch-1 sps)*

Row 89: Ch 1, sc in first dc, [ch 1, sk next cl, sc in next ch-1sp] 19 times, ch 1, sk next cl, sc in 3rd ch of beg ch-3, turn. *(21 sc, 20 ch-1 sps)*

Row 90: Ch 3, [cl in next ch-1 sp, ch 1] 19 times, cl in next ch-1 sp, dc in last sc, turn. *(20 cl, 2 dc, 19 ch-1 sps)*

Rows 91–116: [Rep rows 89 and 90 alternately] 27 times.

Row 117: Rep row 89. At end of row, fasten off.

ASSEMBLY

Join Panels tog with Panel 2 in center and 1 Panel 1 at each side.

To join Panels, hold 2 Panels WS tog and long edge at top, working through both thicknesses at same time, join white with sc in end of first row at right-hand edge, working across side in ends of rows, work [sc, ch 1] evenly spaced across. Fasten off. Join rem Panel in same manner.

EDGING

Rnd 1 (RS): Hold piece with RS facing and beg ch to right, join pink in end of row 1, ch 1, sc in same sp, working across side in ends of row, work [ch 1, sc] 85 times evenly spaced across to next corner ch-2 sp, (sc, ch 1, sc) in corner sp *(corner)*, working across next side in unused lps of beg ch and ch-1 sps, sc in first lp, work [ch 1, sc] 60 times evenly spaced across to next corner ch-2 sp, (sc, ch 1, sc) in corner sp *(corner)*, working across side in ends of row, sc in first row, work [ch 1, sc] 85 times evenly spaced across to next corner ch-2 sp, (sc, ch 1, sc) in corner sp *(corner)*, working across next side in sc and in ch-1 sps, sc in first sc, work [ch 1, sc] 60 times evenly spaced across to next corner ch-2 sp, (sc, ch 1, sc) in corner sp *(corner)*, join in beg sc. *(302 sc, 294 ch-1 sps)*

Rnd 2: Ch 2 *(see Pattern Notes)*, *hdc in each sc and ch-1 sp across to next corner ch-1 sp, (hdc, ch 2, hdc) in corner ch-1 sp *(corner)*, rep from * 3 times, join in 2nd ch of beg ch-2. Fasten off. *(600 hdc, 4 ch-2 sps)*

Rnd 3: Join white in lower left corner, ch 1, (sc, ch 1, sc) in same sp *(corner)*, *ch 1, sk next hdc, sc in next hdc, rep from * across to next corner, ch 1, sk next hdc, (sc, ch 2, sc) in next ch-2 sp *(corner)*, **ch 1, sk next hdc, sc in next hdc, rep from ** across to corner, ch 1, sk next hdc, (sc, ch 2, sc) in next ch-2 sp *(corner)*, *** (ch 1, sk next hdc, sc in next hdc, rep from *** across to next corner ch-2 sp, ch 1, (sc, ch 2, sc) in corner ch-2 sp *(corner)*, ****ch 1, sk next hdc, sc in next hdc, rep from **** across to beg sc, ch 1, join in beg sc.

Rnd 4: Ch 6 *(see Pattern Notes)*, [tr cl *(see Special Stitches)* in next 3 ch-1 sps, ch 4] 29 times, **tr dec** *(see Stitch Guide)* in next ch-1 sp and in corner ch-2 sp, ch 2, (tr, ch 1, tr, ch 1, tr) in same corner ch-2 sp *(corner)*, ch 2, [tr cl in next 3 ch-1 sps, ch 4] 20 times, tr cl in next 3 ch-1 sps, ch 2, (tr, ch 1, tr, ch 1, tr) in next corner ch-2 sp *(corner)*, ch 2, tr dec in same ch-2 sp and in next ch-1 sp, ch 2, [tr cl in next 3 ch-1 sps, ch 4] 28 times, tr cl in next 3 ch-1 sps, ch 2, [tr, ch 1] 4 times in next corner ch-2 sp, tr in same sp *(corner)*, ch 2, [tr cl in next 3 ch-1 sps, ch 4] 20 times, tr cl in next 3 ch-1 sps, ch 2, [tr, ch 1] 4 times in next corner ch-2 sp, join in 4th ch of beg ch-6.

Rnd 5: Sl st in next ch-2 sp, (sc, **picot** *(see Special Stitches)*, sc) in same sp, ch 1, (2 picots, ch 1) in each of next 29 ch-4 sps, (sc, picot, sc) in each of next 4 ch sps, ch 1, (2 picots, ch 1) in each of next 20 ch-4 sps, (sc, picot, sc) in each of next 5 ch sps, (2 picot, ch 1) in each of next 28 ch-4 sps, (sc picot, sc) in each of next 6 ch sps, ch 1, (2 picots, ch 1) in each of next 20 ch-4 sps, (sc, picot, sc) in each of next 5 ch sps, join in beg sc. Fasten off. ∎

Christening Blanket

Design by Darla Sims

SKILL LEVEL
◼◼◼◻ INTERMEDIATE

FINISHED SIZE
40 x 40 inches

MATERIALS

- Lion Brand Baby Soft light (light worsted) weight yarn (4 oz/ 367 yds/113g per ball):
    6 balls #200 white pompadour
- Sizes G/6/4mm and H/8/6mm crochet hooks or size needed to obtain gauge
- Tapestry needle
- 4 yds ¼-inch white satin ribbon

GAUGE
With size H hook: shell = 1½ inches; 5 rows = 2½

PATTERN NOTES
Weave in ends as work progresses.

Join with a slip stitch unless otherwise stated.

Chain-3 at beginning of double crochet rows/ rounds count as first double crochet unless otherwise stated.

Chain-4 at beginning of double crochet rows count as first double crochet and chain-1 space unless otherwise stated.

Chain-6 at beginning of double crochet rounds count as first double crochet and chain-3 space unless otherwise stated.

SPECIAL STITCH
Shell: 5 dc in st indicated.

INSTRUCTIONS
Row 1 (RS): With size H hook, ch 131, sc in 6th ch from hook *(beg 5 sk chs count as first dc and 2 sk chs)*, sk next 2 chs, *shell *(see Special Stitch)* in next ch, sk next 2 chs, sc in next ch, ch 3, sk next 2 chs, sc in next ch, sk next 2 chs, rep from * to last 7 chs, shell in next ch, sk next 2 chs, sc in next ch, ch 1, sk next 2 chs, dc in last ch, turn. *(14 shells, 28 sc, 13 ch–3 sps, 2 dc)*

Row 2: Ch 1, sc in first dc, *dc in each of next 2 dc, ch 3, sc in next dc, ch 3, dc in each of next 2 dc, sc in next ch-3 sp, rep from * 13 times, dc in each of next 2 dc, ch 3, sc in next ch-3 sp, ch 3, dc in each of next 2 dc, sc in 3rd ch of beg 5 sk chs, turn.

Row 3: Ch 3 *(see Pattern Notes)*, 2 dc in first sc, sc in next ch-3 sp, ch 3, sc in next ch-3 sp, *shell in next sc, sc in next ch-3 sp, ch 3, sc in next ch-3 sp, rep from * 12 times, 3 dc in last sc, turn.

Row 4: Ch 1, sc in first dc, ch 3, dc in each of next 2 dc, sc in next ch-3 sp, *dc in each of next 2 dc, ch 3, sc in next dc, ch 3, dc in each of next 2 dc, sc in next ch-3 sp, rep from * 12 times, ch 3, sc in 3rd ch of beg ch-3, turn.

Row 5: Ch 4 *(see Pattern Notes)*, sc in next ch-3 sp, *shell in next sc, sc in next ch-3 sp, ch 3, sc in next ch-3 sp, rep from * 13 times, shell in next sc, sc in next ch-3 sp, ch 1, dc in last sc, turn.

Continued on page 117

Old MacDonald's Farm

Design by Ramona B. Chebli

SKILL LEVEL

 INTERMEDIATE

FINISHED SIZE

60 x 61 inches

MATERIALS

- Fine (sport) weight yarn:
  35 oz/3,150 yds/990g white
  3 oz/270 yds/85g each bright
  yellow, light brown, green, dark
  brown, pink, black, dark gray,
  off-white
- Caron Simply Soft medium
  (worsted) weight yarn (3 oz/165
  yds/85g per skein):
  1 skein #2710 gray heather
- Medium (worsted) weight yarn:
  3 oz/150 yds/85g each light gray
  and orange
- Size F/5/3.75mm crochet hook
  or size needed to obtain gauge
- Tapestry needle

GAUGE

4 sc = 1 inch; 4 sc rows = 1 inch

PATTERN NOTES

Weave in ends as work progresses.

Join with a slip stitch unless otherwise stated.

Chain-3 at beginning of double crochet
rounds count as first double crochet unless
otherwise stated.

SPECIAL STITCH

Cluster (cl): Holding back last lp of each dc
on hook, 2 dc in indicated st, yo and draw
through all 3 lps on hook.

INSTRUCTIONS

GIRAFFE BLOCK

Row 1 (WS): With white, ch 47, sc in 2nd ch
from hook, sc in each rem ch across, turn. *(46 sc)*
Row 2 (RS): Ch 1, sc in each sc, turn.
Rows 3–5: Rep row 2.
Rows 6–48: Rep row 2, **changing colors** *(see
Stitch Guide)* as indicated on Giraffe chart.
At end of row 48, fasten off.

Border

Rnd 1 (RS): Hold piece with RS facing and
row 48 at top, join yellow in first sc in upper
right-hand corner, ch 1, (2 sc, ch 1, 2 sc) in
same sc *(corner)*, sc in each of next 44 sc, (2
sc, ch 1, sc) in next sc *(corner)*, working across
next side in ends of rows, work 45 sc evenly
spaced across to next corner, working across
next side in unused lps of beg ch, (2 sc, ch 1,
2 sc) in first lp *(corner)*, sc in each of next 44
unused lps, (2 sc, ch 1, sc) in last lp *(corner)*,
working across next side in ends of rows,
work 45 sc evenly spaced across to beg sc, join
in beg sc. Fasten off. *(188 sc, 4 ch-1 sps)*
Rnd 2: Join green in any corner ch-1 sp, **ch 3**
(see Pattern Notes), (dc, ch 2, **cl**—*see Special
Stitch)* in same sp *(beg corner)*, *ch 1, [cl in
next sc, ch 1, sk next sc] 24 times, (cl, ch 2, cl)
in corner ch-1 sp *(corner)*, rep from * twice,
ch 1, [cl in next sc, ch 1, sk next sc] 24 times,

join in 3rd ch of beg ch-3. Fasten off. *(102 cl, 2 dc, 4 ch-2 sps, 100 ch-1 sps)*

Rnd 3: Join yellow in any corner ch-2 sp, ch 3, (dc, ch 2, cl) in same sp *(beg corner)*, *ch 1, cl in next ch-1 sp, rep from * across to next corner ch-2 sp, (cl, ch 2, cl) in corner ch-2 sp *(corner)*, **ch 1, cl in next ch-1 sp, rep from ** across to next corner ch-2 sp, (cl, ch 2, cl) in corner ch-2 sp *(corner)*, ***ch 1, cl in next ch-1 sp, rep from *** across to next corner ch-2 sp, (cl, ch 2, cl) in corner ch-2 sp *(corner)*, ****ch 1, cl in next ch-1 sp, rep from **** across to beg ch-3, join in 3rd ch of beg ch-3. Fasten off. *(108 cl, 4 ch-2 sps, 100 ch-1 sps)*

CAMEL BLOCK

Row 1 (WS): With white, ch 47, sc in 2nd ch from hook, sc in each rem ch across, turn. *(46 sc)*
Row 2 (RS): Ch 1, sc in each sc, turn.
Rows 3–48: Rep row 2, changing color as indicated on Camel chart. At end of row 48, fasten off.

Border
Work same as Border of Giraffe Block.

KOALA BLOCK

Row 1 (WS): With white, ch 47, sc in 2nd ch from hook, sc in each rem ch across, turn. *(46 sc)*
Row 2 (RS): Ch 1, sc in each sc, turn.
Rows 3–48: Rep row 2, changing color as indicated on Koala chart. At end of row 48, fasten off.

Border
Work same as Border of Giraffe Block.

DOG BLOCK

Row 1 (WS): With white, ch 47, sc in 2nd ch from hook, sc in each rem ch across, turn. *(46 sc)*
Row 2 (RS): Ch 1, sc in each sc, turn.
Rows 3–48: Rep row 2, changing color as indicated on Dog chart. At end of row 48, fasten off.

Border
Work same as Border of Giraffe Block.

BUNNY BLOCK

Row 1 (WS): With white, ch 47, sc in 2nd ch from hook, sc in each rem ch across, turn. *(46 sc)*
Row 2 (RS): Ch 1, sc in each sc, turn.
Rows 3–48: Rep row 2, changing color as indicated on Bunny chart. At end of row 48, fasten off.

Border
Work same as Border of Giraffe Block.

LAMB BLOCK

Row 1 (WS): With white, ch 47, sc in 2nd ch from hook, sc in each rem ch across, turn. *(46 sc)*
Row 2 (RS): Ch 1, sc in each sc, turn.
Rows 3–48: Rep row 2, changing color as indicated on Lamb chart. At end of row 48, fasten off.

Border
Work same as Border of Giraffe Block.

RHINOCEROS BLOCK

Row 1 (WS): With white, ch 47, sc in 2nd ch from hook, sc in each rem ch across, turn. *(46 sc)*
Row 2 (RS): Ch 1, sc in each sc, turn.
Rows 3–48: Rep row 2, changing color as indicated on Rhinoceros chart. At end of row 48, fasten off.

Border
Work same as Border of Giraffe Block.

HIPPO BLOCK

Row 1 (WS): With white, ch 47, sc in 2nd ch from hook, sc in each rem ch across, turn. *(46 sc)*
Row 2 (RS): Ch 1, sc in each sc, turn.
Rows 3–48: Rep row 2, changing color as indicated on Hippo chart. At end of row 48, fasten off.

Border
Work same as Border of Giraffe Block.

KANGAROO BLOCK

Row 1 (WS): With white, ch 47, sc in 2nd ch from hook, sc in each rem ch across, turn. *(46 sc)*

Row 2 (RS): Ch 1, sc in each sc, turn.
Rows 3–48: Rep row 2, changing color as indicated on Kangaroo chart. At end of row 48, fasten off.

Border
Work same as Border of Giraffe Block.

CAT BLOCK
Row 1 (WS): With white, ch 47, sc in 2nd ch from hook, sc in each rem ch across, turn. *(46 sc)*
Row 2 (RS): Ch 1, sc in each sc, turn.
Rows 3–48: Rep row 2, changing color as indicated on Cat chart. At end of row 48, fasten off.

Border
Work same as Border of Giraffe Block.

COW BLOCK
Row 1 (WS): With white, ch 47, sc in 2nd ch from hook, sc in each rem ch across, turn. *(46 sc)*
Row 2 (RS): Ch 1, sc in each sc, turn.
Rows 3–48: Rep row 2, changing color as indicated on Cow chart. At end of row 48, fasten off.

Border
Work same as Border of Giraffe Block.

MOUSE BLOCK
Row 1 (WS): With white, ch 47, sc in 2nd ch from hook, sc in each rem ch across, turn. *(46 sc)*
Row 2 (RS): Ch 1, sc in each sc, turn.
Rows 3–48: Rep row 2, changing color as indicated on Mouse chart. At end of row 48, fasten off.

Border
Work same as Border of Giraffe Block.

PONY BLOCK
Row 1 (WS): With white, ch 47, sc in 2nd ch from hook, sc in each rem ch across, turn. *(46 sc)*

Row 2 (RS): Ch 1, sc in each sc, turn.
Rows 3–48: Rep row 2, changing color as indicated on Pony chart. At end of row 48, fasten off.

Border
Work same as Border of Giraffe Block.

LION BLOCK
Row 1 (WS): With white, ch 47, sc in 2nd ch from hook, sc in each rem ch across, turn. *(46 sc)*
Row 2 (RS): Ch 1, sc in each sc, turn.
Rows 3–48: Rep row 2, changing color as indicated on Lion chart. At end of row 48, fasten off.

Border
Work same as Border of Giraffe Block.

ELEPHANT BLOCK
Row 1 (WS): With white, ch 47, sc in 2nd ch from hook, sc in each rem ch across, turn. *(46 sc)*
Row 2 (RS): Ch 1, sc in each sc, turn.
Rows 3–48: Rep row 2, changing color as indicated on Elephant chart. At end of row 48, fasten off.

Border
Work same as Border of Giraffe Block.

PIG BLOCK
Row 1 (WS): With white, ch 47, sc in 2nd ch from hook, sc in each rem ch across, turn. *(46 sc)*
Row 2 (RS): Ch 1, sc in each sc, turn.
Rows 3–48: Rep row 2, changing color as indicated on Pig chart. At end of row 48, fasten off.

Border
Work same as Border of Giraffe Block.

Continued on page 117

Buttercream Afghan

Design by Kim Guzman

SKILL LEVEL

 ■■■□ EXPERIENCED

FINISHED SIZE
40 x 50 inches

MATERIALS
- Fine (sport) weight 55% nylon/ 45% acrylic yarn: **2 FINE**
  21 oz/1,890 yds/594g butter yellow
- Size G/6/4mm crochet hook or size needed to obtain gauge
- Tapestry needle
- Stitch markers

GAUGE
Motif = 9 inches across straight edge and 6½" from straight edge to top

PATTERN NOTES
Weave in ends as work progresses.

Join with a slip stitch unless otherwise stated.

Chain-3 at beginning of double crochet rounds count as first double crochet unless otherwise stated.

SPECIAL STITCHES
Beginning linked single crochet (beg linked sc): Insert hook in indicated st, yo, draw lp through, insert hook in next st, yo, draw lp through, yo and draw through all 3 lps on hook.
Linked single crochet (linked sc): Insert hook in side of indicated st, yo, draw lp through, insert hook in next st, yo, draw lp through, yo and draw through all 3 lps on hook.

INSTRUCTIONS

MOTIF
Make 14.
Row 1 (RS): Ch 5, join in first ch to form ring, sl st in ring, **ch 3** *(see Pattern Notes)*, (5 dc, ch 3, 6 dc) in ring, turn. *(12 dc, 1 ch-3 sp)*
Row 2: Ch 3, dc in first dc, dc in each of next 5 dc, ch 1, (3 dc, ch 3, 3 dc) in next ch-3 sp, ch 1, dc in each of next 5 dc, 2 dc in 3rd ch of beg ch-3, turn. *(20 dc, 1 ch-3 sp)*
Row 3: Ch 3, dc in first dc, dc in each of next 6 dc, ch 3, (3 dc, ch 3, 3 dc) in next ch-3 sp, ch 3, sk next 3 dc, dc in each of next 6 dc, 2 dc in 3rd ch of beg ch-3, turn. *(22 dc, 3 ch-3 sps)*
Row 4: Ch 3, dc in first dc, dc in each of next 7 dc, ch 3, sk next ch-3 sp, (3 dc, ch 3, 3 dc, ch 3, 3 dc) in next ch-3 sp, ch 3, sk next 3 dc, dc in each of next 7 dc, 2 dc in 3rd ch of beg ch-3, turn. *(27 dc, 4 ch-3 sps)*
Row 5: Ch 3, dc in first dc, dc in each of next 8 dc, sk next ch-3 sp, *ch 3, (3 dc, ch 3, 3 dc) in next ch-3 sp, rep from * once, ch 3, sk next 3 dc, dc in each of next 8 dc, 2 dc in 3rd ch of beg ch-3, turn. *(32 dc, 5 ch-3 sps)*
Row 6: Ch 3, dc in first dc, dc in each of next 9 dc, sk next ch-3 sp, *ch 2, (3 dc, ch 3, 3 dc) in next ch-3 sp, rep from * twice, ch 2, sk next 3 dc, dc in each of next 9 dc, 2 dc in 3rd ch of beg ch-3, ch 3, turn. *(40 dc, 3 ch-3 sps, 4 ch-2 sps)*

Row 7: Ch 3, dc in first dc, dc in each of next 10 dc, [ch 3, (3 dc, ch 3, 3 dc) in next ch-3 sp] 3 times, ch 3, sk next 3 dc, dc in each of next 10 dc, 2 dc in 3rd ch of beg ch-3, turn. *(42 dc, 7 ch-3 sps)*

Row 8: Ch 3, dc in first dc, dc in each of next 11 dc, *ch 2, sk next ch-3 sp, 9 dc in next ch-3 sp, rep from * twice, ch 2, sk next 3 dc, dc in each of next 11 dc, 2 dc in 3rd ch of beg ch-3, ch 3, turn. *(53 dc, 4 ch-2 sps)*

Row 9: Ch 3, dc in first dc, dc in each of next 12 dc, *[dc in next dc, ch 1] 8 times, dc in next dc, rep from * twice, dc in each of next 12 dc, 2 dc in 3rd ch of beg ch-3, ch 1, working across next side in ends of rows, work 38 sc evenly spaced across. Fasten off. *(55 dc, 25 ch-1 sps)*

BORDER

Note: Motifs are joined to form Border. Before joining last Motif to first Motif, be sure Motifs are not twisted.

Hold 1 Motif with RS facing and straight edge at top, join yarn in first sc, ch 1, sc in same sc *(mark sc)*, sc in each of next 37 sc, *hold next Motif with RS and straight edge at top, sc in each sc across Motif, rep from * once, ch 1 *(corner)*, **hold next Motif with RS and straight edge at top, sc in each sc across Motif, rep from ** 3 times, ch 1 *(corner)*, ***hold next Motif with RS and straight edge at top, sc in each sc across Motif, rep from *** twice, ch 1 *(corner)*, ****hold next Motif with RS and straight edge at top, sc in each sc across Motif, rep from **** 3 times, ch 1 *(corner)*, join in beg sc.

BODY

Row 1 (RS): Ch 114, **beg linked sc** *(see Special Stitches)* in 2nd and 3rd chs from hook, ***linked sc** *(see Special Stitches)* in previous st and in next ch, rep from * across, turn. *(112 linked sc)*

Row 2: Ch 2, beg linked sc in 2nd ch from hook and in next st, *linked sc in previous st and in next st, rep from * across, turn.

Rows 3–80: Rep row 2.

Edging

Rnd 1: Ch 1, 3 sc in first st *(corner)*, work 112 sc evenly spaced across to last st, 3 sc in last st *(corner)*, working across next side in ends of rows, work 150 sc evenly spaced across, working across next side in unused lps of beg ch, 3 sc in first ch *(corner)*, work 112 evenly spaced across to last ch, 3 sc in last ch *(corner)*, working across next side in ends of rows, work 150 sc evenly spaced to beg sc, join in beg sc.

Note: On following rnd, Body is joined to Border.

Rnd 2: Sl st in each of next 2 sc, ch 1, hold Border with RS facing, sl st in marked sc on Border, *ch 1, sk next sc on rnd 1, sl st in next sc, ch 1, sk next sc on Border, sl st in next sc of Border, rep from * 55 times, ch 1, sk next 2 sc on rnd 1, sl st in next sc, ch 1, sk next ch-1 sp on Border, sl st in first sc on next Motif, **ch 1, sk next sc on rnd 1, sl st in next sc, ch 1, sk next sc on Border, sl st in next sc of Border, rep from ** 74 times, ch 1, sk next 2 sc on rnd 1, sl st in next sc, ch 1, sk next ch-1

sp on Border, sl st in first sc on next Motif, ***ch 1, sk next sc on rnd 1, sl st in next sc, ch 1, sk next sc on Border, sl st in next sc of Border, rep from *** 55 times, ch 1, sk next 2 sc on rnd 1, sl st in next sc, ch 1, sk next ch-1 sp on Border, sl st in first sc on next Motif, ****ch 1, sk next sc on rnd 1, sl st in next sc, ch 1, sk next sc on Border, sl st in next sc of Border, rep from **** 74 times, ch 1, join in 2nd beg sl st. Fasten off.

CORNER MOTIF
Make 4.
Note: Work Corner Motif between Motifs at each marked corner. For proper placement of sl sts on following rows, dc are counted from top down on sides of Motifs.

Row 1 (RS): Hold Body with RS facing and 1 marked corner ch-1 sp of Border at top, join yarn in 13th dc on side of Motif to right of marked sp, ch 1, (3 dc, ch 3, 3 dc) in marked ch-1 sp, ch 1, sk 14th dc on Motif to left, sl st in each of next 3 dc on same Motif, turn. *(6 dc, 1 ch-3 sp, 2 ch-1 sps)*

Row 2: Ch 1, (3 dc, ch 3, 3 dc, ch 3, 3 dc) in next ch-3 sp, ch 1, sl st in 11th dc on side of first Motif, sl st in each of next 2 dc on same Motif, turn. *(9 dc, 2 ch-3 sps, 2 ch-1 sps)*

Row 3: Ch 3, [(3 dc, ch 3, 3 dc) in ch-3 sp, ch 3] twice, sl st in 9th dc on side of opposite Motif, sl st in next 2 dc of same Motif, turn. *(12 dc, 5 ch-3 sps)*

Row 4: Ch 2, [(3 dc, ch 3, 3 dc) in ch-3 sp, ch 2] 3 times, sl st in 7th dc on side of first Motif, sl st in next 2 dc of same Motif, turn. *(18 dc, 3 ch-3 sps, 2 ch-2 sps)*

Row 5: Ch 3, [(3 dc, ch 3, 3 dc) in ch-3 sp, ch 3] 3 times, sl st in 5th dc on side of opposite Motif, sl st in next 2 dc of same Motif, turn. *(18 dc, 7 ch-3 sps)*

Row 6: Ch 2, [sk next ch-3 sp, 9 dc in next ch-3 sp, ch 2] 3 times, sl st in 3rd dc on side of first Motif, sl st in next 2 dc of same Motif, turn. *(27 dc, 4 ch-1 sps)*

Row 7: *[Dc in next dc, ch 1] 8 times, dc in next dc, rep from * twice, sl st in first dc on opposite Motif. Fasten off. *(27 dc, 24 ch-1 sps)*

FILLER MOTIF
Make 10.
Note: Work Filler Motif in each rem sp between Motifs. For proper placement of sl sts on following rows, dc are counted from top down on sides of Motifs.

Row 1: Hold Body with RS facing, join yarn with sl st in 13th dc in side of Motif to right, ch 3, sk 14th dc on side of Motif to left, sl st in each of next 3 dc on same Motif, turn. *(1 ch-3 sp)*

Row 2: Ch 1, (3 dc, ch 3, 3 dc) in next ch-3 sp, ch 1, sl st in 11th dc on side of first Motif, sl st in each of next 2 dc on same Motif, turn. *(6 dc, 1 ch-3 sp, 2 ch-1 sps)*

Row 3: Ch 1, (3 dc, ch 3, 3 dc, ch 3, 3 dc) in next ch-3 sp, ch 1, sl st in 9th dc on side of opposite Motif, sl st in each of next 2 dc on same Motif, turn. *(9 dc, 2 ch-3 sps, 2 ch-1 sps)*

Row 4: Ch 2, [(3 dc, ch 3, 3 dc) in next ch-3 sp, ch 2] twice, sl st in 7th dc on side of first Motif, sl st in each of next 2 dc on same Motif, turn. *(12 dc, 2 ch-3 sps, 3 ch-2 sps)*

Row 5: Ch 3, [(3 dc, ch 3, 3 dc) in next ch-3 sp, ch 3] twice, sl st in 5th dc on side of opposite Motif, sl st in each of next 2 dc on same Motif, turn. *(12 dc, 5 ch-3 sps)*

Row 6: Ch 2, sk next ch-3 sp, [9 dc in next ch-3 sp, ch 2] twice, sl st in 3rd dc on side of first Motif, sl st in each of next 2 dc on same Motif, turn. *(18 dc, 3 ch-2 sps)*

Row 7: *[Dc in next dc, ch 1] 8 times, dc in next dc, rep from * once, sl st in first dc on opposite Motif. Fasten off. *(18 dc, 16 ch-1 sps)*

EDGING
Join yarn in first ch-1 sp of any 9-dc group, ch 1, sc in same sp, [ch 3, sc in next ch-1 sp] 7 times, *sc in next ch-1 sp, [ch 3, sc in next ch-1 sp] 7 times, rep from * around, join in beg sc. Fasten off. ∎

RING AROUND THE ROSIE BABY AFGHAN

Continued from page 100

PLAIN HEXAGON

Make 24.

Rnd 1 (RS): Ch 4, join in first ch to form a ring, **ch 3**, 2 dc in ring, ch 2, *3 dc in ring, ch 2, rep from * 4 times, join in 3rd ch of beg ch-3. *(18 dc, 6 ch-3 sps)*

Rnd 2: Ch 3, *ch 1, sk next dc, 2 dc in next dc, ch 1, sk next dc, (2 dc, ch 2, 2 dc) in next ch-2 sp, rep from * 4 times, ch 1, sk next dc, 2 dc in next dc, ch 1, sk next dc, (2 dc, ch 2, dc) in next ch-2 sp, join in 3rd ch of beg ch-3. *(36 dc, 6 ch-2 sps, 12 ch-1 sps)*

Rnd 3: Sl st in next ch-1 sp, ch 3, dc in same sp, ch 1, 2 dc in next ch-1 sp, ch 1, *(2 dc, ch 2, 2 dc) in next ch-2 sp, ch 1, [2 dc in next ch-1 sp, ch 1] twice, rep from * 4 times, (2 dc, ch 2, 2 dc) in next ch-2 sp, join in 3rd ch of beg ch-3. *(48 dc, 6 ch-2 sps)*

Rnd 4: Sl st in next dc, sl st in next ch-1 sp, ch 3, dc in same sp, ch 1, 2 dc in next ch-1 sp, ch 1, *(2 dc, ch 2, 2 dc) in next ch-2 sp, ch 1, [2 dc in next ch-1 sp, ch 1] 3 times, rep from * 4 times, (2 dc, ch 2, 2 dc) in next ch-2 sp, ch 1, 2 dc in next ch-1 sp, ch 1, join in 3rd ch of beg ch-3. *(60 dc, 6 ch-2 sps, 24 ch-1 sps)*

Rnd 5: Sl st in next dc, sl st in next ch-1 sp, ch 3, dc in same sp, ch 1, 2 dc in next ch-1 sp, ch 1, (2 dc, ch 2, 2 dc) in next ch-2 sp, *ch 1, [2 dc in next ch-1 sp, ch 1] 4 times, (2 dc, ch 2, 2 dc) in next ch-2 sp, rep from * 4 times, ch 1, [2 dc in next ch-1 sp, ch 1] twice, join in 3rd ch of beg ch 3. *(72 dc, 6 ch-2 sps, 30 ch-1 sps)*

Rnd 6: Sl st in next dc, sl st in next ch-1 sp, ch 3, dc in same sp, ch 1, 2 dc in next ch-1 sp, ch 1, (2 dc, ch 2, 2 dc) in next ch-2 sp, *ch 1, [2 dc in next ch-1 sp, ch 1] 5 times, (2 dc, ch 2, 2 dc) in next ch-2 sp, rep from * 4 times, ch 1, [2 dc in next ch-1 sp, ch 1] 3 times, join in 3rd ch of beg ch-3. Fasten off. *(84 dc, 6 ch-2 sps, 36 ch-1 sps)*

ASSEMBLY

Referring to diagram for placement and with tapestry needle and matching yarn color, sew Blocks tog.

BORDER

Hold piece with RS facing, join pink with sc in any ch-2 sp, sc in same sp, working around entire piece, sc in each sc and 2 sc in each ch-2 sp around, join in beg sc. ∎

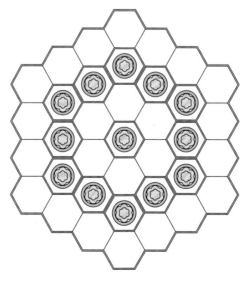

Ring Around the Rosie
Assembly Diagram

CHRISTENING BLANKET
Continued from page 106

Row 6: Ch 1, sc in first dc, *dc in each of next 2 dc, ch 3, sc in next dc, ch 3, dc in each of next 2 dc, sc in next ch-3 sp, rep from * to last ch-1 sp, sk last ch-1 sp, sc in 3rd ch of beg ch-4, turn.

Rep rows 3–6 until piece measures 35 inches from beg, ending with row 5. At end of last row, fasten off.

BORDER

Rnd 1 (RS): Holding piece with RS facing, with size G hook, join yarn with sc in upper right-hand corner, 2 sc in same sp *(beg corner)*, *work 124 sc evenly spaced to next corner, 3 sc in corner *(corner)*, rep from * 3 times, work 124 sc evenly spaced to beg sc, join in beg sc. *(508 sc)*

Rnd 2: Ch 1, sc in same sc as joining, *ch 4, sk next sc, sc in next sc, ch 2, sc in next sc, [ch 4, sk next 2 sc, sc in next sc, ch 2, sk next

sc, sc in next sc] 24 times, ch 4, sk next 2 sc, sc in next sc, ch 2 **, sc in next sc, rep from * 3 times, ending last rep at **, join in beg sc.

Rnd 3: Sl st in next ch-4 sp, ch 3, 6 dc in same sp, sc in next ch-2 sp, *7 dc in next ch-4 sp, sc in next ch-2 sp, rep from * around, join in 3rd ch of beg ch-3.

Rnd 4: Ch 4, *dc in next dc, ch 1, rep from * around, join in 3rd ch of beg ch-4.

Rnd 5: Ch 6 *(see Pattern Notes)*, *dc in next dc, ch 3, rep from * around. **Do not join.**

Rnd 6: 4 sc in sp formed by beg ch-6, 4 sc in each ch-3 sp around, join in beg sc. Fasten off.

FINISHING

Cut ribbon into sixteen 9-inch lengths. Tie each length to Blanket at evenly spaced intervals and tie into bows. ∎

OLD MACDONALD'S FARM
Continued from page 111

Old MacDonald's Farm
Assembly Diagram

ASSEMBLY
Referring to assembly diagram for placement and with yellow, sew Blocks tog.

BORDER
Hold piece with RS facing, join green in any corner ch-2 sp, ch 3, (sl st, ch 3, sl st) in same sp, *(sl st, ch 4, cl) in next ch-1, sk next ch-1 sp, rep from * across to next corner ch-2 sp, (sl st, ch 3) twice in corner ch-2 sp, sl st in same sp, **(sl st, ch 4, cl) in next ch-1, sk next ch-1 sp, rep from ** across to next corner ch-2 sp, (sl st, ch 3) twice in corner ch-2 sp, sl st in same sp, ***(sl st, ch 4, cl) in next ch-1, sk next ch-1 sp, rep from *** across to next corner ch-2 sp, (sl st, ch 3) twice in corner ch-2 sp, sl st in same sp, ****(sl st, ch 4, cl) in next ch-1, sk next ch-1 sp, rep from **** across to joining sl st, join in joining sl st. Fasten off. ∎

Charts continued on the next page

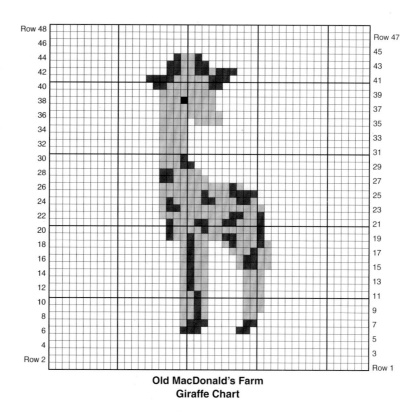

Old MacDonald's Farm
Giraffe Chart

COLOR KEY
- ☐ White
- ☐ Off-White
- ☐ Tan
- ☐ Brown
- ■ Dark Brown
- ☐ Light Gray
- ☐ Dark Gray
- ☐ Grey Heather
- ■ Black
- ☐ Pink

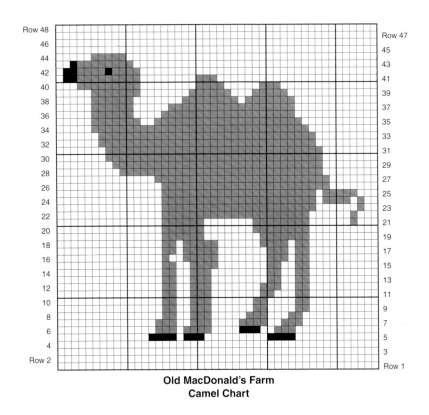

**Old MacDonald's Farm
Camel Chart**

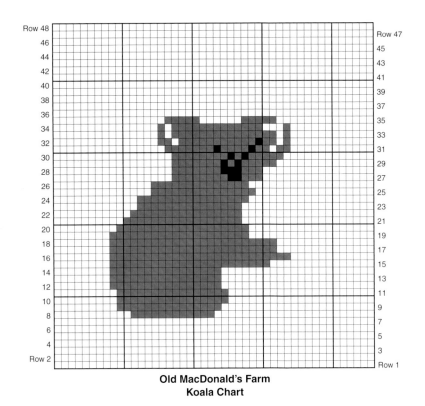

**Old MacDonald's Farm
Koala Chart**

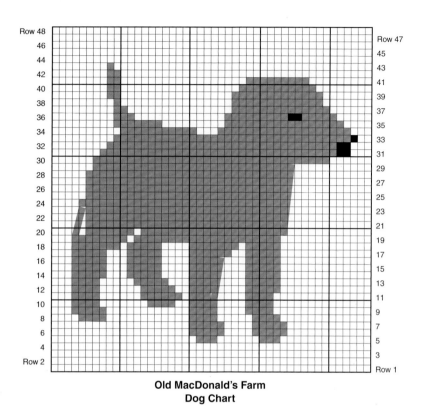

**Old MacDonald's Farm
Dog Chart**

COLOR KEY
☐ White
☐ Off-White
▨ Tan
▨ Brown
■ Dark Brown
▨ Light Gray
▨ Dark Gray
▨ Grey Heather
■ Black
▨ Pink

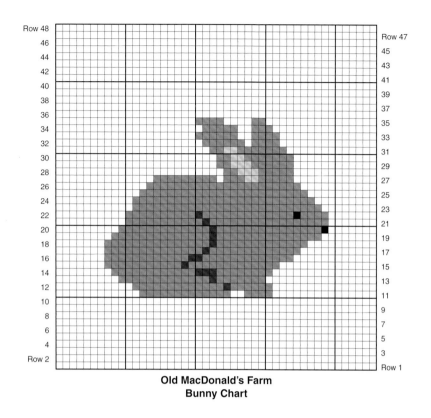

**Old MacDonald's Farm
Bunny Chart**

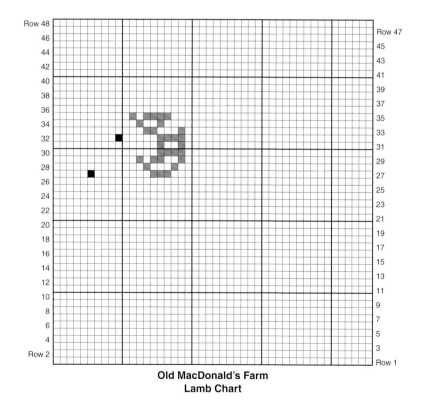

**Old MacDonald's Farm
Lamb Chart**

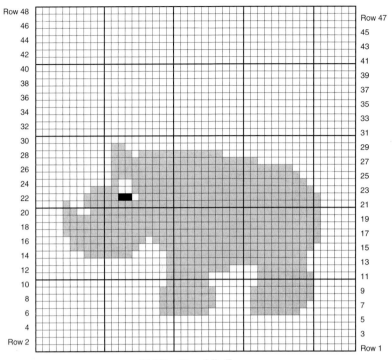

**Old MacDonald's Farm
Rhinoceros Chart**

COLOR KEY
☐ White
☐ Off-White
▨ Tan
▨ Brown
▪ Dark Brown
▨ Light Gray
▨ Dark Gray
▨ Grey Heather
▪ Black
▨ Pink

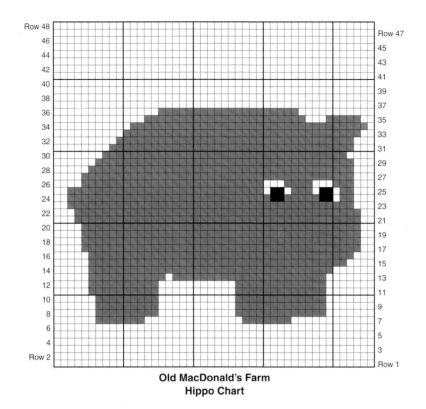

**Old MacDonald's Farm
Hippo Chart**

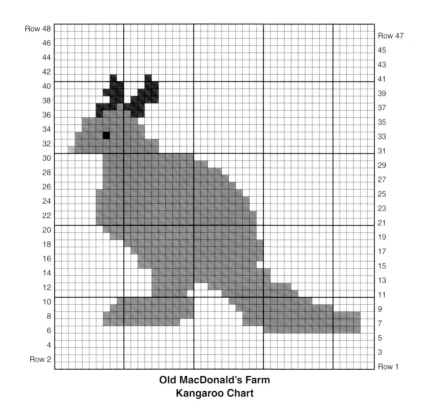

**Old MacDonald's Farm
Kangaroo Chart**

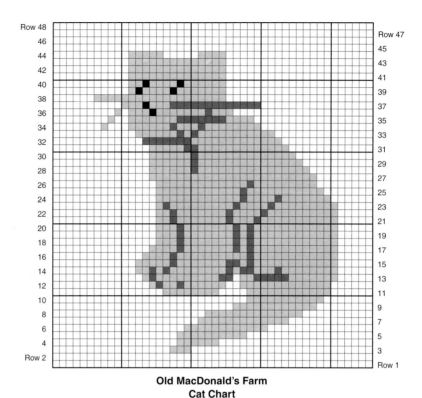

**Old MacDonald's Farm
Cat Chart**

COLOR KEY
☐ White
☐ Off-White
▨ Tan
▨ Brown
■ Dark Brown
▨ Light Gray
▨ Dark Gray
▨ Grey Heather
■ Black
▨ Pink

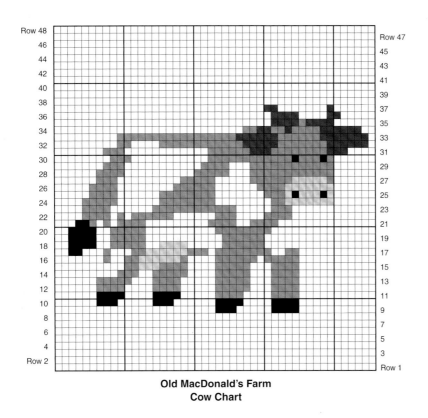

**Old MacDonald's Farm
Cow Chart**

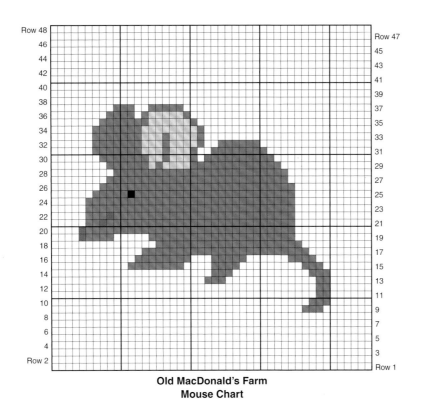

**Old MacDonald's Farm
Mouse Chart**

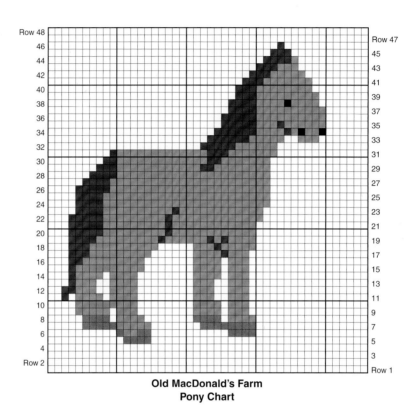

Row 48 | Row 47
46 | 45
44 | 43
42 | 41
40 | 39
38 | 37
36 | 35
34 | 33
32 | 31
30 | 29
28 | 27
26 | 25
24 | 23
22 | 21
20 | 19
18 | 17
16 | 15
14 | 13
12 | 11
10 | 9
8 | 7
6 | 5
4 | 3
Row 2 | Row 1

**Old MacDonald's Farm
Pony Chart**

COLOR KEY
- ☐ White
- ☐ Off-White
- Tan
- Brown
- Dark Brown
- Light Gray
- Dark Gray
- Grey Heather
- Black
- Pink

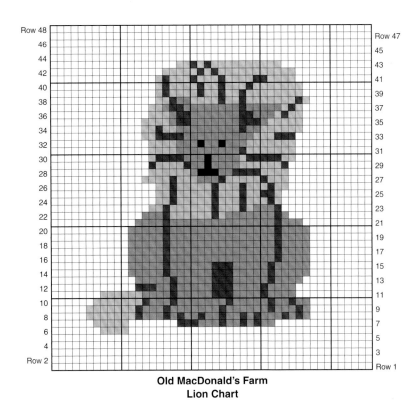

**Old MacDonald's Farm
Lion Chart**

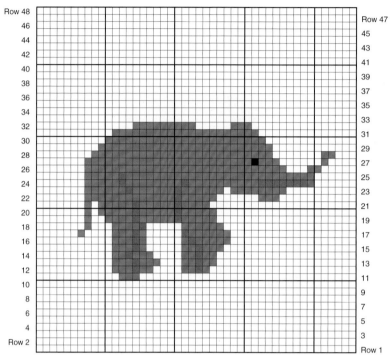

Row 48 · 46 · 44 · 42 · 40 · 38 · 36 · 34 · 32 · 30 · 28 · 26 · 24 · 22 · 20 · 18 · 16 · 14 · 12 · 10 · 8 · 6 · 4 · Row 2

Row 47 · 45 · 43 · 41 · 39 · 37 · 35 · 33 · 31 · 29 · 27 · 25 · 23 · 21 · 19 · 17 · 15 · 13 · 11 · 9 · 7 · 5 · 3 · Row 1

**Old MacDonald's Farm
Elephant Chart**

COLOR KEY
- ☐ White
- ☐ Off-White
- ☐ Tan
- ☐ Brown
- ■ Dark Brown
- ☐ Light Gray
- ☐ Dark Gray
- ☐ Grey Heather
- ■ Black
- ☐ Pink

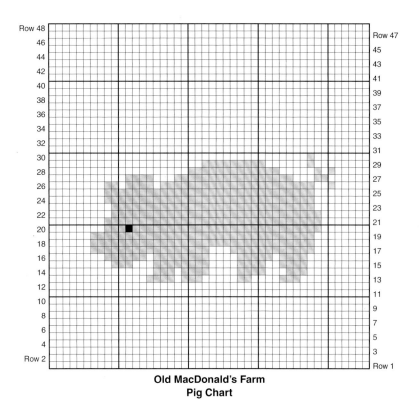

**Old MacDonald's Farm
Pig Chart**

Hope Chest Treasures

Every girl should have a hope chest to keep items in for her wedding day. These afghan treasures are pretty but practical as they will be used for many years to come.

Blue Ice

Design by Judy Teague Treece

SKILL LEVEL

■ ■ □ □ EASY

FINISHED SIZE

56 x 64 inches

MATERIALS

- Red Heart Super Saver medium (worsted) weight yarn (7 oz/ 364 yds/198g per skein):
    8 skeins #365 coffee
    1 skein #381 light blue
- Red Heart Classic medium (worsted) weight yarn (3½ oz/190yds/99g per skein):
    7 skeins #882 country blue
- Size H/8/5mm crochet hook or size needed to obtain gauge
- Tapestry needle

GAUGE

Rnds 1 & 2 = 2½ inches
Square = 7¾ inches

PATTERN NOTES

Weave in ends as work progresses.

Join with a slip stitch unless otherwise stated.

Chain-3 at beginning of double crochet rounds counts as first double crochet unless otherwise stated.

INSTRUCTIONS

SQUARE

Make 56.

Rnd 1 (RS): With light blue, ch 4, join in first ch to form ring, **ch 3** *(see Pattern Notes),* 4 dc in ring, ch 1, [5 dc in ring, ch 1] 3 times, join in 3rd ch of beg ch-3. Fasten off. *(20 dc, 4 ch-1 sps)*

Rnd 2: Join country blue in any ch-1 sp, ch 3, (dc, ch 2, 2 dc) in same sp *(beg corner),* dc in each of next 5 dc, *(2 dc, ch 2, 2 dc) in next ch-1 sp *(corner),* dc in each of next 5 dc, rep from * twice, join in 3rd ch of beg ch-3. *(36 dc, 34 ch-2 sps)*

Rnd 3: Sl st in next dc, sl st in next ch-2 sp, ch 3, (dc, ch 2, 2 dc) in same sp *(beg corner),* *dc in each of next 2 dc, **fptr** *(see Stitch Guide)* around next dc 2 rows below, sk dc behind fptr, dc in each of next 3 dc, fptr around next dc 2 rows below, sk dc behind fptr, dc in each of next 2 dc, (2 dc, ch 2, 2 dc) in next ch-2 sp *(corner),* rep from * twice, dc in each of next 2 dc, fptr around next dc 2 rows below, sk dc behind fptr, dc in each of next 2 dc, fptr around next dc 2 rows below, sk dc behind fptr, dc in each of next 2 dc, join in 3rd ch of beg ch-3. Fasten off. *(8 fptr, 44 dc, 4 ch-2 sps)*

Rnd 4: Join brown in any corner ch-2 sp, ch 3, (dc, ch 2, 2 dc) in same sp *(beg corner),* dc in each of next 2 dc, [fptr around next dc 2 rows below, sk dc behind fptr, dc in each of next 3 sts] twice, fptr around next dc 2 rows

Continued on page 150

Connecticut Waved Cables

Design by Joyce Nordstrom

SKILL LEVEL

 INTERMEDIATE

FINISHED SIZE
52 x 60 inches

MATERIALS
- Red Heart Soft Yarn medium (worsted) weight yarn (solids: 5 oz/256 yds/140g per skein; prints: 4 oz/204 yds/113g per skein):
  - 3 skeins #4601 off-white
  - 2 skeins each #1882 toast and #9344 chocolate
  - 1 skein each #9275 paprika, #9543 embers
- Size I/9/5.5mm crochet hook or size needed to obtain gauge
- Tapestry needle

GAUGE
7 sts = 2 inches; 6 rows = 2 inches
Strip = 5¼ inches wide at widest point

PATTERN NOTES
Weave in ends as work progresses.

Chain-3 at beginning of double crochet rows counts as first double crochet unless otherwise stated.

On working row, skip stitch behind each front post stitch.

SPECIAL STITCH
Crossed post stitch (crossed post st): Yo, sk next indicated st, insert hook from front to back to front around hdc 1 row below, yo, [draw through 2 lps on hook] twice, yo, insert hook from front to back to front around sk st 1 row below, yo, [draw through 2 lps on hook] twice.

INSTRUCTIONS

PANEL A
Make 4.

Row 1 (WS): With off-white, ch 18, hdc in 3rd ch from hook, hdc in each rem ch across, turn. *(16 hdc)*

Row 2 (RS): Ch 2, hdc in each of first 3 hdc, **fphdc** *(see Stitch Guide)* around each of next 2 hdc, hdc in each of next 6 hdc, fphdc around each of next 2 hdc, hdc in each of next 3 hdc, turn.

Row 3: Ch 2, hdc in each st across, turn.

Row 4: Ch 2, hdc in each of first 3 hdc, fphdc around each of next 2 fphdc 1 row below, hdc in each of next 2 hdc, **crossed post st** *(see Special Stitch)* around next 2 sts 1 row below, hdc in each of next 2 hdc, fphdc around each of next 2 fphdc 1 row below, hdc in each of last 3 hdc, turn.

Row 5: Rep row 3.

Row 6: Ch 2, hdc in first hdc, **hdc dec** *(see Stitch Guide)* in next 2 sts, hdc in next hdc, fphdc around each of next 2 fphdc 1 row below, hdc in each of next 4 hdc, fphdc around each of next 2 fphdc 1 row below, hdc in next hdc, hdc dec in next 2 sts, hdc in last hdc, turn. *(14 sts)*

Row 7: Rep row 3.

Row 8: Ch 2, hdc in first hdc, hdc dec in next 2 sts, hdc in next hdc, fphdc around each of next 2 fphdc 1 row below, hdc in each of next 2 hdc, fphdc around each of next 2 fphdc 1 row below, hdc in next hdc, hdc dec in next 2 hdc, hdc in last hdc, turn. *(12 sts)*

Row 9: Rep row 3.

Row 10: Ch 2, hdc in first hdc, hdc dec in next 2 sts, hdc in next hdc, fphdc around each of next 4 sts 1 row below, hdc in next hdc, hdc dec in next 2 hdc, hdc in last hdc, turn. *(10 sts)*

Row 11: Rep row 3.

Row 12: Ch 2, hdc in each of first 3 hdc, sk next 2 fphdc, **fptr** *(see Stitch Guide)* around each of next 2 sts 1 row below, fptr around each of next 2 sts 1 row below, sk next st, hdc in each of last 3 hdc, turn. *(10 sts)*

Row 13: Rep row 3.

Row 14: Ch 2, hdc in first hdc, 2 hdc in next st, fphdc around each of next 2 sts 1 row below, hdc in each of next 2 hdc, fphdc

around each of next 2 sts 1 row below, 2 hdc in next st, hdc in last hdc, turn. *(12 sts)*

Row 15: Rep row 3.

Row 16: Ch 2, hdc in first hdc, 2 hdc in next hdc, fphdc around each of next 2 sts 1 row below, hdc in each of next 4 hdc, fphdc around each of next 2 sts 1 row below, 2 hdc in next st, hdc in last hdc, turn. *(14 sts)*

Row 17: Rep row 3.

Row 18: Ch 2, hdc in first hdc, 2 hdc in next hdc, fphdc around each of next 2 sts 1 row below, hdc in each of next 6 hdc, fphdc around each of next 2 sts 1 row below, 2 hdc in next hdc, hdc in last hdc, turn. *(16 sts)*

Row 19: Rep row 3.

Rows 20–147: [Rep rows 4–19 consecutively] 8 times.

Row 148: Rep row 4.

Row 149: Rep row 3.

Row 150: Rep row 2.

Row 151: Rep row 3.

Edging

Ch 1, (sc, ch 2, sc) in first st *(corner)*, *sc in next st, ch 1, sk next st, rep from * across to last st, (sc, ch 2, sc) in last st *(corner)*, working across next side in ends of rows, **sc in next row, ch 1, rep from ** to next corner, working across next side in unused lps of beg ch, (sc, ch 2, sc) in first lp *(corner)*, ***sc in next lp, ch 1, sk next lp, rep from *** across to last lp, (sc, ch 2, sc) in last lp *(corner)*, working across next side in ends of rows, ****sc in next row, ch 1, rep from **** to beg sc, join in beg sc. Fasten off.

PANEL B
Make 2.
With chocolate, work same as Panel A.

PANEL C
Make 1.
Row 1 (WS): With off-white, ch 12, dc in 3rd ch from hook, hdc in each rem ch across, turn. *(10 hdc)*

Row 2 (RS): Ch 2, dc in each of first 3 hdc, fphdc around each of next 4 hdc 1 row below, hdc in each of next 3 hdc, turn. *(10 sts)*

Row 3: Ch 2, hdc in each st across, turn.
Row 4: Ch 2, hdc in each of first 3 hdc, sk next 2 fphdc, fptr around each of next 2 sts, fptr around each of 2 sk sts, sk next st, hdc in last 3 hdc, turn. *(10 sts)*
Row 5: Rep row 3.
Row 6: Ch 2, hdc in first hdc, 2 hdc in next st, fphdc around each of next 2 sts, hdc in each of next 2 hdc, fphdc around each of next 2 sts, 2 hdc in next st, hdc in last hdc, turn. *(12 sts)*
Row 7: Rep row 3.
Row 8: Ch 2, hdc in first hdc, 2 hdc in next hdc, fphdc around each of next 2 sts, hdc in each of next 4 hdc, fphdc around each of next 2 sts, 2 hdc in next st, hdc in last hdc, turn. *(14 sts)*
Row 9: Rep row 4.
Row 10: Ch 2, hdc in first hdc, 2 hdc in next hdc, fphdc around each of next 2 sts, hdc in each of next 6 hdc, fphdc around each of next 2 sts, 2 hdc in next hdc, hdc in last hdc, turn. *(16 sts)*
Row 11: Rep row 3.
Row 12: Ch 2, hdc in each of first 3 hdc, fphdc around each of next 2 fphdc 1 row below, hdc in each of next 2 hdc, crossed post st around next 2 sts 1 row below, hdc in each of next 2 hdc, fphdc around each of next fphdc 1 row below, hdc in each of last 3 hdc, turn.
Row 13: Rep row 3.
Row 14: Ch 2, hdc in first hdc, hdc dec in next 2 sts, hdc in next hdc, fphdc around each of next 2 fphdc 1 row below, hdc in each of next 4 hdc, fphdc around each of next 2 fphdc 1 row below, hdc in next hdc, hdc dec in next 2 sts, hdc in last hdc, turn. *(14 sts)*
Row 15: Rep row 3.
Row 16: Ch 2, hdc in first hdc, hdc dec in next 2 sts, hdc in next hdc, fphdc around each of next 2 fphdc 1 row below, hdc in each of next 2 hdc, fphdc around each of next 2 fphdc 1 row below, hdc in next hdc, hdc dec in next 2 sts, hdc in last hdc, turn. *(12 sts)*
Row 17: Rep row 3.
Row 18: Ch 2, hdc in first hdc, hdc dec in next 2 sts, hdc in next hdc, fphdc around each of next 4 sts 1 row below, hdc in next

hdc, hdc dec in next 2 hdc, hdc in last hdc, turn. *(10 sts)*
Row 19: Rep row 3.
Row 20: Ch 2, hdc in each of first 3 hdc, sk next 2 fphdc, fptr around each of next 2 sts 1 row below, fptr around each of next 2 sts 1 row below, sk next st, hdc in each of last 3 hdc, turn. *(10 sts)*
Row 21: Rep row 3.
Row 22: Ch 2, hdc in first hdc, 2 hdc in next st, fphdc around each of next 2 sts 1 row below, hdc in each of next 2 hdc, fphdc around each of next 2 sts 1 row below, 2 hdc in next st, hdc in last hdc, turn. *(12 sts)*
Row 23: Rep row 3.
Row 24: Ch 2, hdc in first hdc, 2 hdc in next hdc, fphdc around each of next 2 sts 1 row below, hdc in each of next 4 hdc, fphdc around each of next 2 sts 1 row below, 2 hdc in next st, hdc in last hdc, turn. *(14 sts)*
Row 25: Rep row 3.
Row 26: Ch 2, hdc in first hdc, 2 hdc in next hdc, fphdc around each of next 2 sts 1 row below, hdc in each of next 6 hdc, fphdc around each of next 2 sts 1 row below, 2 hdc in next hdc, hdc in last hdc, turn. *(16 sts)*
Row 27: Rep row 3.
Rows 28–139: [Rep rows 12–27 consecutively] 8 times.
Rows 140–149: Rep rows 12–21.
Row 150: Rep row 2.
Row 151: Rep row 4.

Edging
Work same as Edging of Panel A.

PANEL D
Make 2.
With toast, work same as Panel C.

PANEL E
Make 2.
With chocolate, work same as Panel C.

PANEL E
Make 2.
With paprika, work same as Panel C.

Continued on page 151

Diamonds in the Sky

Design by Dorothy Warrell

SKILL LEVEL

 EASY

FINISHED SIZE

48 x 68 inches

MATERIALS

- TLC Essentials medium (worsted) weight yarn (6 oz/312 yds/ 170g per skein):
    7 skeins #2820 robin egg
- Size H/8/5mm crochet hook or size needed to obtain gauge
- Tapestry needle

GAUGE

Rnds 1 & 2 = 3 inches
Block = 9 inches

PATTERN NOTES

Weave in ends as work progresses.

Join with a slip stitch unless otherwise stated.

Chain-3 at beginning of double crochet rounds counts as first double crochet unless otherwise stated.

Chain-5 at beginning of double crochet rounds counts as first double crochet and chain-2 space unless otherwise stated.

INSTRUCTIONS

BLOCK

Make 35.

Rnd 1 (RS): Ch 6, join in first ch to form ring, **ch 3** *(see Pattern Notes)*, 23 dc in ring, join in 3rd ch of beg ch-3. **Turn.** *(24 dc)*

Rnd 2: Ch 3, *dc in each of next 2 dc, ch 1, sk next dc, dc in each of next 2 dc, (dc, ch 3, dc) in next dc *(corner)*, rep from * twice, dc in each of next 2 dc, ch 1, sk next dc, dc in each of next 2 dc, dc in same st as beg ch-3, ch 3, join in 3rd ch of beg ch-3. Turn. *(24 dc, 4 ch–3 sps, 4 ch–1 sps)*

Rnd 3: Ch 3, *(2 dc, ch 3, 2 dc) in next corner ch-3 sp *(corner)*, dc in each of next 3 dc, dc in next ch-1 sp **, dc in each of next 3 dc, rep from * 3 times, ending last rep at **, dc in each of next 2 dc, join in 3rd ch of beg ch-3. Turn. *(44 dc, 4 ch–3 sps)*

Rnd 4: Ch 3, dc in each of next 2 dc, ch 1, sk next dc, dc in each of next 5 dc, *(2 dc, ch 3, 2 dc) in next corner ch-2 sp *(corner)*, dc in each of next 5 dc, ch 1, sk next dc, dc in each of next 5 dc, rep from * twice, (2 dc, ch 3, 2 dc) in next corner ch-2 sp *(corner)*, dc in each of next 2 dc, join in 3rd ch of beg ch-3. Turn. *(56 dc, 4 ch–3 sps, 4 ch–1 sps)*

Rnd 5: Ch 3, dc in each of next 4 dc, *(2 dc, ch 3, 2 dc) in next corner ch-2 sp *(corner)*, dc in each of next 7 dc, dc in next ch-1 sp, dc in each of next 7 dc, dc in next ch-1 sp **, dc in each of next 7 dc, rep from * 3 times, ending last rep at **, dc in each of next 2 dc, join in

Continued on page 151

Poodle Afghan

Design by Holly Fields

SKILL LEVEL

 INTERMEDIATE

FINISHED SIZE
40 x 52 inches

MATERIALS
- Caron Simply Soft medium (worsted) weight yarn (6 oz/ 330 yds/170g per skein):
    - 4 skeins #9722 plum wine
    - 2 skeins each #9701 white and #9727 black
- Caron Bliss bulky (chunky) weight yarn (1¾ oz/71 yds/50g per skein):
    - 1 skein each #0001 snow and #0013 black
- Size H/8/5mm crochet hook or size needed to obtain gauge
- Tapestry needle
- Sewing needle
- 2 yds ¼-inch wide mauve satin ribbon
- Mauve sewing thread

GAUGE
5 sc = 1 inch; 5 sc rows = 1 inch

PATTERN NOTES
Weave in ends as work progresses.

Join with a slip stitch unless otherwise stated.

SPECIAL STITCHES
Shell: 8 dc in indicated place.
Picot: Ch 3, sl st in 3rd ch from hook.

INSTRUCTIONS

SQUARE
Make 6 with snow for poodle section and 6 with black for poodle section.
Row 1 (RS): With plum wine, ch 41, sc in 2nd ch from hook, sc in each rem ch across, turn. *(40 sc)*
Row 2: Ch 1, sc in each sc across, turn.
Rows 3–40: Work according to chart, **changing colors** *(see Stitch Guide)* as indicated on chart and substituting black for snow on 6 squares. At end of last row, **do not fasten off.**

Edging
Rnd 1 (RS): Ch 1, 3 sc in first sc *(corner)*, sc in each sc across to last sc, 3 sc in last sc *(corner)*, working across next side in ends of rows, sc in each row, working across next side in unused lps of beg ch, 3 sc in first lp *(corner)*, sc in each lp across to last lp, 3 sc in last lp *(corner)*, working across next side in ends of rows, sc in each row, join in beg sc. Fasten off. *(168 sc)*
Rnd 2: Hold piece with RS facing, join snow with sc in same sc as joining, 3 sc in next sc *(corner)*, *sc in each sc to 2nd sc of next corner, 3 sc in 2nd sc *(corner)*, rep from * twice, sc in each sc across to beg sc, join in beg sc. Fasten off. *(176 sc)*
Rnd 3: Hold piece with RS facing, join black with sc in same sc as joining, sc in next sc, 3 sc in next sc *(corner)*, *sc in each sc across to 2nd sc of next corner, 3 sc in 2nd sc *(corner)*, rep from * twice, sc in each sc across to beg

sc, join in beg sc. Leaving a 12-inch end, fasten off. *(184 sc)*

SMALL PUFF BALL

Make 12 snow and 12 black.
With Bliss, ch 4 loosely, join in first ch to form a ring, ch 1, sc in each ch around, join in beg sc. Leaving an 8-inch end, fasten off. *(4 sc)*
Matching color of puff balls to poodles, sew 1 ball to each foot of each poodle over sts indicated on chart by dots.

MEDIUM PUFF BALL

Make 6 snow and 6 black.
With Bliss, ch 4 loosely, join with sl st in first ch to form a ring, ch 1, 2 sc in same ch as joining, sc in next sc, 2 sc in next ch, sc in next ch, join in beg sc. Leaving an 8-inch length of yarn, fasten off. *(6 sc)*
Matching color of puff balls to poodles, sew 1 ball to tail of each poodle, over sts indicated on chart by dots.

LARGE PUFF BALL

Make 6 snow and 6 black.
With Bliss, ch 4 loosely, join in first ch to form a ring, ch 1, 2 sc in each ch around, join in beg sc. Fasten off. *(8 sc)*
Matching color of puff balls to poodles, sew 1 ball to head of each poodle over sts indicated on chart by dots.

SQUARE FINISHING

Referring to photo for placement, with black and using French knot *(Fig. 1)*, embroider eye on poodle of each Square.
Cut ribbon in 6-inch lengths and tie each length in bow. Sew bow to large puff ball on each poodle head.

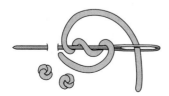

French Knot
Fig. 1

ASSEMBLY

Referring to assembly diagram, sew Squares tog.

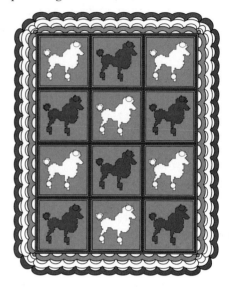

Poodle Afghan
Assembly Diagram

EDGING

Rnd 1 (RS): Hold piece with RS facing and 1 short end at top, join black with sc in 2nd sc of upper right-hand corner, sc in same sc *(beg corner)*, *sc in each sc across to last sc, 3 sc in last sc *(corner)*, rep from * twice, sc in each sc to beg sc, sc in same sc as beg sc, join in beg sc. *(652 sc)*

Rnd 2: Ch 1, 3 sc in same sc *(corner)*, *sc in each sc to 2nd sc of next corner, 3 sc in 2nd sc *(corner)*, rep from * 3 times, sc in each sc to beg sc, join in beg sc. Fasten off. *(660 sc)*

Rnd 3: Join plum wine with sc in 2nd sc of first corner, sc in same sc *(beg corner)*, *sc in each sc across to 2nd sc of next corner, 3 sc in 2nd sc *(corner)*, rep from * twice, sc in each sc to beg sc, sc in same sc as beg sc, join in beg sc. *(668 sc)*

Rnd 4: Ch 1, 3 sc in same sc *(corner)*, *sc in each sc to 2nd sc of next corner, 3 sc in 2nd sc *(corner)*, rep from * 3 times, sc in each sc to beg sc, join in beg sc. *(676 sc)*

Rnd 5: Ch 1, sc in next sc, *ch 5, sk next 3 sc, sc in next sc, rep from * across to 2nd sc of next corner, ch 3, (sc, ch 3, sc) in 2nd sc *(corner)*, **ch 5, sk next 3 sc, sc in next sc, rep from ** across to 2nd sc of next corner, ch 3, (sc, ch 3, sc) in 2nd sc *(corner)*, ***ch 5, sk next 3 sc, sc in next sc, rep from *** across to 2nd sc of next corner, ch 3, (sc, ch 3, sc) in 2nd sc *(corner)*, ****ch 5, sk next 3 sc, sc in next sc, rep from **** across to beg sc, join in beg sc. *(168 ch-5 sps, 4 ch-3 sps)*

Rnd 6: Ch 1, sc in next ch-5 sp, **shell** *(see Special Stitches)* in next ch-5 sp, sc in next ch-5 sp, *ch 5, sc in next ch-5 sp, shell in next ch-5 sp, sc in next ch-5 sp, rep from * across to next ch-3 sp, ch 1, (dc, ch 1, dc) in next ch-3 sp, ch 1, (dc, ch 1, dc) in next ch-3 sp, ch 1, sc in next ch-5 sp, shell in next ch-5 sp, sc in next ch-5 sp, **ch 5, sc in next ch-5 sp, shell in next ch-5 sp, sc in next ch-5 sp, rep from ** across to next ch-3 sp, ch 1, (dc, ch 1, dc) in next ch-3 sp, ch 1, (dc, ch 1, dc) in next ch-3 sp, ch 1, sc in next ch-5 sp, shell in next ch-5 sp, sc in next ch-5 sp, ***ch 5, sc in next ch-5 sp, shell in next ch-5 sp, sc in next ch-5 sp, rep from *** across to next ch-3 sp, ch 1, (dc, ch 1, dc) in next ch-3 sp, ch 1, (dc, ch 1, dc) in next ch-3 sp, ch 1, sc in next ch-5 sp, shell in next ch-5 sp, sc in next ch-5 sp, ****ch 5, sc in next ch-5 sp, shell in next ch-5 sp, sc in next ch-5 sp, rep from ** across to beg sc, join in beg sc. *(56 shells)*

Rnd 7: Ch 1, dc in first dc, [**picot** *(see Special Stitches)*, dc in next dc] 7 times, *sc in next ch-5 sp, sk next sc, dc in next dc, [picot, dc in next dc] 7 times, rep from * across to next ch-1 sp, sc in next ch-1 sp, ch 1, [dc, ch 1] twice in each of next 3 ch-1 sps, sc in last ch-1 sp, sk next sc, dc in next dc, [picot, dc in next dc] 7 times, **sc in next ch-5 sp, sk next sc, dc in next dc, [picot, dc in next dc] 7 times, rep from ** across to next ch-1 sp, sc in next ch-1 sp, ch 1, [dc, ch 1] twice in each of next 3 ch-1 sps, sc in last ch-1 sp, sk next sc, dc in next dc, [picot, dc in next dc] 7 times, ***sc in next ch-5 sp, sk next sc, dc in next dc, [picot, dc in next dc] 7 times, rep from *** across to next ch-1 sp, sc in next ch-1 sp, ch 1, [dc, ch 1] twice in each of next 3 ch-1 sps, sc in last ch-1 sp, sk next sc, dc in next dc, [picot, dc in next dc] 7 times, ****sc in next ch-5 sp, sk next sc, dc in next dc, [picot, dc in

next dc] 7 times, rep from **** across to last sp, join in last sp. Fasten off.

Rnd 8: Join white with sc in same sp as joining, *ch 5, sk next 2 picots, sc in next picot, ch 5, sk next picot, sc in next picot, ch 5, sk next 2 picots, sk next dc, dc in next sc, rep from * across to next ch-1 sp, sc in each of first 3 ch-1 sps of corner, (sc, ch 3) twice in next ch-1 sp, sc in same sp, sc in each of last 3 ch-1 sps, dc in next sc, **ch 5, sk next 2 picots, sc in next picot, ch 5, sk next picot, sc in next picot, ch 5, sk next 2 picots, sk next dc, dc in next sc, rep from ** across to next ch-1 sp, sc in each of first 3 ch-1 sps of corner, (sc, ch 3) twice in next ch-1 sp, sc in same sp, sc in each of last 3 ch-1 sps, dc in next sc, ***ch 5, sk next 2 picots, sc in next picot, ch 5, sk next picot, sc in next picot, ch 5, sk next 2 picots, sk next dc, dc in next sc, rep from * across to next ch-1 sp, sc in each of first 3 ch-1 sps of corner, (sc, ch 3) twice in next ch-1 sp, sc in same sp, sc in each of last 3 ch-1 sps, dc in next sc, ****ch 5, sk next 2 picots, sc in next picot, ch 5, sk next picot, sc in next picot, ch 5, sk next 2 picots, sk next dc, dc in next sc, rep from * across to beg sc, join in beg sc.

Rnd 9: Ch 5, sc in next ch-5 sp, shell in next ch-5 sp, sc in next ch-5 sp, *ch 5, sc in next ch-5 sp, shell in next ch-5 sp, sc in next ch-5 sp, rep from * across to next corner, ch 5, (dc, ch 1, dc) in first corner sp, ch 1, (dc, ch 1, dc) in 2nd corner sp, ch 5, sc in next ch-5 sp, shell in next ch-5 sp, sc in next ch-5 sp, **ch 5, sc in next ch-5 sp, shell in next ch-5 sp, sc in next ch-5 lp, rep from ** across to next corner, ch 5, (dc, ch 1, dc) in first corner sp, ch 1, (dc, ch 1, dc) in 2nd corner sp, ch 5, sc in next ch-5 sp, shell in next ch-5 sp, sc in next ch-5 sp, ***ch 5, sc in next ch-5 sp, shell in next ch-5 sp, sc in next ch-5 sp, rep from *** across to next corner, ch 5, (dc, ch 1, dc) in first corner sp, ch 1, (dc, ch 1, dc) in 2nd corner sp, ****ch 5, sc in next ch-5 sp, shell in next ch-5 sp, sc in next ch-5 sp, rep from **** across to beg ch-5, ch 5, join in beg ch-5 sp.

Continued on page 152

Pineapples & Lace

Design by Bettie Dowler & Dorotha Shappie

SKILL LEVEL

 INTERMEDIATE

FINISHED SIZE

48 x 66 inches

MATERIALS

- Medium (worsted) weight yarn:
  38 oz/1,900 yds/1,075g mauve
- Size H/8/5mm crochet hook or size
  needed to obtain gauge
- Tapestry needle

GAUGE

(5 dc, 2 cl, 5 chs) = 2¾ inches; 3 pattern rows =
2 inches

PATTERN NOTES

Weave in ends as work progresses.

Chain-4 at beginning of double crochet rows
counts as first double crochet and chain-1
space unless otherwise stated.

SPECIAL STITCHES

Cluster (cl): Holding back last 2 lps of each
dc on hook, 2 dc in indicated st, yo and draw
through all 5 lps on hook.

V-stitch (V-st): (Dc, ch 1, dc) in indicated sp.

INSTRUCTIONS

AFGHAN
Body
Row 1 (RS): Ch 106, (4 dc, ch 2, dc) in 7th
ch from hook, *ch 1, sk next 3 chs, (**cl** *(see*

Special Stitches), ch 2, cl) in next ch, sk next
3 chs, (4 dc, ch 2, dc) in next ch, rep from *
across to last 3 chs, sk next 2 chs, dc in last
ch, turn.
Row 2: Ch 3, *(4 dc, ch 2, dc) in next ch-2 sp,
ch 1, (cl, ch 2, cl) in next ch-2 sp, rep from
* across ending with (4 dc, ch 2, dc) in last
ch-2 sp, ch 1, dc in top of beg ch, turn.
Rows 3–78: Rep row 2. **Do not fasten off** at
end of last row.

Edging
Ch 1, 3 sc in corner st *(corner)*, work 100
sc evenly spaced across, 3 sc in next corner
(corner), working across next side in ends of
rows, work 232 sc evenly spaced across, 3
sc in corner lp *(corner)*, work 100 sc evenly
spaced across to next corner, 3 sc in corner
(corner), working across next side in ends of
rows, work 232 sc evenly spaced across to beg
sc, join in beg sc. Fasten off. *(676 sc)*

PINEAPPLE
Make 30.
Row 1 (RS): Ch 5, join with sl st in first ch to
form a ring, ch 4 *(see Pattern Notes)*, (dc, ch
1, dc, ch 1, dc) in ring, turn. *(4 dc, 3 ch-1 sps)*
Row 2: Ch 5, V-st *(see Special Stitches)* in
each of next 3 ch-1 sps, turn. *(3 V-sts,
1 ch-5 sp)*
Row 3: Ch 5, V-st in ch-1 sp of next V-st, ch
1, (2 dc, ch 3, 2 dc) in next ch-1 sp, ch 1, V-st
in ch-1 sp of next V-st, turn. *(2 V-sts, 4 dc, 1
ch-5 sp, 1 ch-3 sp, 2 ch-1 sps)*

Continued on page 153

Floral Fantasy

Design by Lori Zeller

SKILL LEVEL
■■■■ EXPERIENCED

FINISHED SIZE
38 x 52 inches

MATERIALS
• Caron Simply Soft medium (worsted) weight yarn (6 oz/ 330yds/170g per skein):
  3 skeins #9702 off-white
  2 skeins each #9719 soft pink, #9717 orchid and #9705 sage
  1 skein #9726 soft yellow
• Size I/9/5.5mm crochet hook or size needed to obtain gauge
• Tapestry needle
• Stitch markers

GAUGE
Rnds 1–3 = 4 inches in diameter

PATTERN NOTES
Weave in ends as work progresses.

Join with a slip stitch unless otherwise stated.

Chain-3 at beginning of double crochet rounds counts as first double crochet unless otherwise stated.

Chain-4 at beginning of double crochet rounds counts as first double crochet and chain-1 space unless otherwise stated.

SPECIAL STITCHES
Beginning shell (beg shell): Ch 4, (dc, ch 1) 4 times in indicated sp, dc in same sp.
Shell: (Dc, ch 1) 5 times in indicated sp, dc in same sp.
Beginning corner shell (beg corner shell): Ch 3, (dc, ch 3, 2 dc) in indicated place.
Corner shell: (2 dc, ch 3, 2 dc) in indicated place.
V-stitch (V-st): (Dc, ch 1, dc) in indicated place.

INSTRUCTIONS

SQUARE
Make 12.
Inner Square
Rnd 1: With soft yellow, ch 5, join in first ch to form ring, ch 2, 16 dc in ring, **join** in first dc. Fasten off. *(16 dc)*
Rnd 2: Join pink with sc in any dc, 2 sc in next dc, [sc in next dc, 2 sc in next dc] 7 times, join in **front lp** *(see Stitch Guide)* of beg sc. *(24 sc)*
Rnd 3: Ch 1, sc in same sp, working in front lps only, (dc, tr, dtr) in next sc, (dtr, tr, dc) in next sc, *sc in next sc, (dc, tr, dtr) in next sc, (dtr, tr, dc) in next sc, rep from * 6 times, join in beg sc. Fasten off. *(16 dtr, 16 tr, 16 dc, 8 sc)*
Rnd 4: Join sage with sc in unused **back lp** *(see Stitch Guide)* of first sc of rnd 2, ch 3, sk next 2 sc on rnd 2, *sc in back lp of next sc on rnd 2, ch 3, sk next 2 sc on rnd 2, rep from * 6 times, join in beg sc. *(8 sc, 8 ch-3 sps)*
Rnd 5: Sl st in next ch-3 sp, ch 2, sc in same sp, ch 2, (sc, ch 3, tr, ch 3, sl st in last tr, tr,

ch 3, sc) in next ch-3 sp *(leaf)*, ch 2, *(sc, ch 2, sc) in next ch-3 sp, ch 2, (sc, ch 3, tr, ch 3, sl st in last tr, tr, ch 3, sc) in next ch-3 sp *(leaf)*, ch 2, rep from * twice, join in beg sc. Fasten off. *(4 leaves)*

Rnd 6: Join off-white with sc in first ch-2 sp on rnd 5, ch 5, sc in same sp, ch 3, sc in next ch-2 sp, ch 3, working behind next leaf, sc in next ch-2 sp, ch 3, *(sc, ch 5, sc) in next ch-3 sp, ch 3, sc in next ch-2 sp, ch 3, working behind next leaf, sc in next ch-2 sp, ch 3, rep from * around, join in first sc.

Rnd 7: Sl st in next ch-5 sp, **beg shell** *(see Special Stitches)* in same sp, [ch 2, sc in next ch-3 sp] 3 times, ch 2, ***shell** (see Special Stitches)* in next ch-5 sp, [ch 2, sc in next ch-3 sp] 3 times, ch 2, rep from * around, join in 3rd ch of beg ch-4. *(4 shells)*

Rnd 8: Sl st in first ch-sp, ch 1, sc in same sp, [ch 3, sc in next ch-1 sp] 4 times, ch 1, sk next ch-2 sp, [**V-st** *(see Special Stitches)* in next ch-2 sp, ch 1] twice, *sc in next ch-3 sp, [ch 3, sc in next ch-1 sp] 4 times, ch 1, sk next ch-2 sp, [V-st in next ch-2 sp, ch 1] twice, rep from * around, join in first sc.

Rnd 9: Sl st in first ch-sp, ch 1, sc in same sp, [ch 3, sc in next ch sp] 5 times, *ch 3, sk next ch-sp, sc in next ch sp, [ch 3, sc in next ch sp] 7 times, rep from * twice, ch 3, sk next ch sp, [sc in next ch sp, ch 3] twice, join in beg sc.

Rnd 10: Sl st in first ch-3 sp, ch 4, dc in same sp, ***corner shell** (see Special Stitches)* in next ch-3 sp, V-st in each of next 7 ch-3 sps, rep from * twice, corner shell in next ch-3 sp, V-st in each of next 6 ch-3 sps, join in 3rd ch of beg ch-4. Fasten off.

Violet insertion
First Violet
Rnd 1: With soft yellow, ch 2, 8 sc in 2nd ch from hook, join in first sc. Fasten off.

Rnd 2: Join orchid with sc in any sc, ch 5, sc in same sc *(beg petal)*, (sc, ch 5, sc) in each of next 5 sc *(5 petals)*, place marker in last ch-5 sp made, (sc, ch 5, sc) in next sc *(petal)*, sc in next sc, ch 2, sl st in ch-3 sp of first corner shell on rnd 10 of Inner Square, ch 2, sc in same st as last sc, join in first sc. Fasten off.

2nd Violet
Rnd 1: Rep rnd 1 of First Violet.

Rnd 2: Join orchid with sc in any sc, ch 5, sc in same sc *(beg petal)*, sc in next sc, ch 2, sl st in marked ch-5 sp on previous Violet, ch 2, sc in same st as last sc, (sc, ch 5, sc) in each of next 4 sc *(4 petals)*, place marker in last ch-5 sp made, (sc, ch 5, sc) in next sc, sc in next sc, ch 2, sl st in ch-1 sp of next V-st of Inner Square, ch 2, sc in same st as last sc, join in beg sc. Fasten off.

3rd Violet
Rnd 1: Rep rnd 1 of First Violet.

Rnd 2: Join orchid with sc in any sc, ch 5, sc in same sc, sc in next st, ch 2, sl st in marked ch-5 sp on previous Violet, ch 2, sc in same st as last sc, (sc, ch 5, sc) in each of next 4 sc, place marker in last ch-5 sp made, (sc, ch 5, sc) in next sc, sc in next sc, ch 2, sk next 2 V-sts on Inner Square, sl st in ch-1 sp of next V-st of Inner Square, ch 2, sc in same st as last sc, join in beg sc of petals. Fasten off.

4th Violet
Work same as 3rd Violet.

5th Violet
Rnd 1: Rep rnd 1 of First Violet.

Rnd 2: Join orchid with sc in any sc of center, ch 5, sc in same sc, sc in next st, ch 2, sl st in marked ch-5 sp of previous Violet, ch 2, sc in same st as last sc, (sc, ch 5, sc) in each of next 4 sc, place marker in last ch-5 sp made, (sc, ch 5, sc) in next sc, sc in next sc, ch 2, sl st in ch-3 sp of next corner shell of Inner Square, ch 2, sc in same st as last sc, join in beg sc of petals. Fasten off.

Sixth Violet
Work same as 2nd Violet.

7th & 8th Violets
Work same as 3rd Violet.

9th Violet
Work same as 5th Violet.

10th Violet
Work same as 2nd Violet.

11th & 12th Violets
Work same as 3rd Violet.

13th Violet
Work same as 5th Violet.

14th Violet
Work same as 2nd Violet.

15th Violet
Work same as 3rd Violet.

16th Violet
Rnd 1: Rep rnd 1 of First Violet.

Rnd 2: Join orchid with sc in any sc of center, ch 5, sc in same sc, sc in next st, ch 2, sl st in marked ch-5 sp of previous Violet, ch 2, sc in same st as last sc, (sc, ch 5, sc) in each of next 3 sc, sc in next st, ch 2, sl st in 2nd ch-5 sp of First Violet, ch 2, sc in same sc as before, (sc, ch 5, sc) in next sc, sc in next sc, ch 2, sk next 2 V-sts on Inner Square, sl st in ch-1 sp of next V-st of Inner Square, ch 2, sc in same st as last sc, join in beg sc of petals. Fasten off.

Edging
Rnd 1: Join sage with sc in back lp of first sc after first unattached ch-5 sp on First Violet from joining to 16th Violet, ch 4, sc in back lp of next sc, ch 2, working behind next ch-5 sp, sc in back lp of next sc, ch 4, sc in back lp of next sc, ch 4, *sc in sc in back lp of sc after first unattached ch-5 sp on next Violet, ch 4, sc in back lp of next sc, ch 2, working behind next ch-5 sp, sc in back lp of next sc, ch 4, sc in back lp of next sc, ch 4, rep from * around, join in beg sc. Fasten off.

Rnd 2: Join off-white in first ch-2 sp on previous rnd, **beg corner shell** *(see Special Stitches)* in same sp, [ch 1, sk next ch-4 sp, 4 dc in next ch-4 sp, ch 1, sk next ch-4 sp, 3 dc in next ch-2 sp] 3 times, ch 1, sk next ch-4 sp, 4 dc in next ch-4 sp, ch 1, *corner shell in next ch-2 sp, [ch 1, sk next ch-4 sp, 4 dc in next ch-4 sp, ch 1, sk next ch-4 sp, 3 dc in

next ch-2 sp] 3 times, ch 1, sk next ch-4 sp, 4 dc in next ch-4 sp, ch 1, rep from * twice, join in 3rd ch of beg ch-3.

Rnd 3: Sl st in next dc and in next ch-3 sp, ch 1, (sc, ch 2, sc) in same sp *(corner)*, ch 3, sc in next ch-4 sp on rnd 1, *ch 3, sk next 2 dc, sc in sp before next dc, [ch 3, sc in next ch-4 sp on rnd 1] twice, rep from * twice, ch 3, sk next 2 dc, sc in sp before next dc, ch 3, sc in next ch-4 sp on rnd 1, ch 3, (sc, ch 2, sc) in next ch-3 sp *(corner)*, ch 3, sc in next ch-4 sp on rnd 1, **ch 3, sk next 2 dc, sc in sp before next dc, [ch 3, sc in next ch-4 sp on rnd 1] twice, rep from ** twice, ch 3, sk next 2 dc, sc in sp before next dc, ch 3, sc in next ch-4 sp on rnd 1, ch 3, (sc, ch 2, sc) in next ch-3 sp *(corner)*, ch 3, sc in next ch-4 sp on rnd 1, ***ch 3, sk next 2 dc, sc in sp before next dc, [ch 3, sc in next ch-4 sp on rnd 1] twice, rep from *** twice, ch 3, sk next 2 dc, sc in sp before next dc, ch 3, sc in next ch-4 sp on rnd 1, ch 3, (sc, ch 2, sc) in next ch-3 sp *(corner)*, ch 3, sc in next ch-4 sp on rnd 1, ****ch 3, sk next 2 dc, sc in sp before next dc, [ch 3, sc in next ch-4 sp on rnd 1] twice, rep from **** twice, ch 3, sk next 2 dc, sc in sp before next dc, ch 3, sc in next ch-4 sp on rnd 1, ch 3, join in beg sc. Fasten off.

Rnd 4: Join soft pink with sc in first corner ch-2 sp made on previous rnd, ch 2, sc in same sp *(beg corner)*, ch 1, working behind sts on rnd 3, dc in each of next 2 dc of corner shell on rnd 2, [ch 1, dc in each of next 2 dc on rnd 2, sk next sc on rnd 3, dc in each of next 2 dc on rnd 2, ch 1, dc in each of next 3 dc on rnd 2] 3 times, ch 1, dc in each of next 2 dc on rnd 2, sk next sc on rnd 3, dc in each of next 2 dc on rnd 2, ch 1, dc in each of next 2 dc on rnd 2, ch 1, *(sc, ch 2, sc) in corner ch-2 sp on rnd 3 *(corner)*, ch 1, dc in each of next 2 dc of corner shell on rnd 2, [ch 1, dc in each of next 2 dc on rnd 2, sk next sc on rnd 3, dc in each of next 2 dc on rnd 2, ch 1, dc in each of next 3 dc on rnd 2] 3 times, ch 1, dc in each of next 2 dc on rnd 2, sk next sc on rnd 3, dc in each of next 2 dc on rnd 2, ch 1, dc in each of next 2 dc on rnd 2, ch 1, rep from * twice, join in beg sc.

Rnd 5: Ch 1, sc in same sc as joining, (sc, ch 2, sc) in next corner ch-2 sp *(corner)*, sc in each dc and ch-1 sp around, working (sc, ch 2, sc) in each rem corner ch-2 sp, join in beg sc. Fasten off.

ASSEMBLY

With tapestry needle and soft pink, sew Squares tog in 4 rows of 3 Squares each.

BORDER

Rnd 1: Hold piece with RS facing, join

off-white with sc in any corner ch-2 sp, 2 sc in same sp *(corner)*, sc in each sc across each square and in each ch sp on both sides of square joinings, and 3 sc in each rem corner ch-2 sp around, join in beg sc. Fasten off.

Rnd 2: Join orchid with sc in any sc, ch 2, sk next sc, *sc in next sc, ch 2, sk next sc, rep from * around, join in beg sc. Fasten off.

Rnd 3: Join off-white with sc in any ch-2 sp, ch 2, *sc in next ch-2 sp, ch 2, rep from * around, join in beg sc. Fasten off. ■

BLUE ICE
Continued from page 132

below, sk dc behind fptr, dc in each of next 2 dc, (2 dc, ch 2, 2 dc) in next corner ch-2 sp *(corner)* **, dc in each of next 2 dc, rep from * 3 times, ending last rep at **, join in 3rd ch of beg ch-3. *(12 fptr, 56 dc, 4 ch–2 sps)*

Rnd 5: Ch 3, dc in next dc, (2 dc, ch 2, 2 dc) in next ch-2 sp *(corner)*, *dc in each st across to next corner ch-2 sp, (2 dc, ch 2, 2 dc) in corner ch-2 sp *(corner)*, rep from * twice, dc in each st across to beg ch-3, join in 3rd ch of beg ch-3. Fasten off. *(84 dc, 4 ch–2 sps)*

Rnd 6: Join country blue in any corner ch-2 sp, (2 sc, ch 2, 2 sc) in same sp *(corner)*, *[ch 1, sk next dc, sc in next dc] 10 times, ch 1, sk next 2 dc, (2 sc, ch 2, 2 sc) in next corner ch-2 sp *(corner)*, rep from * twice, [ch 1, sk next dc, sc in next dc] 10 times, ch 1, join in beg sc. Fasten off. *(56 sc, 4 ch–2 sps, 44 ch–1 sps)*

Rnd 7: Join brown in any corner ch-2 sp, (2 sc, ch 2, 2 sc) in same sp *(corner)*, *[ch 1, sc in next ch-1 sp] 11 times, ch 1, (2 sc, ch 2, 2 sc) in next corner ch-2 sp *(corner)*, rep from * twice, [ch 1, sc in next ch-1 sp] 11 times, ch 1, join in beg sc. Fasten off. *(60 sc, 4 ch–2 sps, 48 ch–1 sps)*

ASSEMBLY

Join Squares tog in 8 rows of 7 Blocks each.

With brown, sl st Squares tog working in **back lps** *(see Stitch Guide)* only.

BORDER

Rnd 1 (RS): Hold piece with RS facing and 1 short end at top, join brown with sc in ch-2 sp in upper right-hand corner, (2 sc, ch 2, 2 sc) in same sp *(corner)*, *ch 1, work (sc in next ch-1 sp, ch 1) across to next corner ch-2 sp, (2 sc, ch 2, 2 sc) in corner ch-2 sp *(corner)*, rep from * twice, ch 1, (sc in next ch-1 sp, ch 1) across to beg sc, join in beg sc.

Rnd 2: Sl st in next sc, sl st in next ch-2 sp, (2 sc, ch 2, 2 sc) in same ch-2 sp *(corner)*, *ch 1, (sc in next ch-1 sp, ch 1) across to next corner ch-2 sp, (2 sc, ch 2, 2 sc) in corner ch-2 *sp (corner)*, rep from * twice, ch 1, (sc in next ch-1 sp, ch 1) across to beg sc, join in beg sc.

Rnd 3: Sl st in next sc, sl st in next ch-2 sp, (2 sc, ch 2, 2 sc) in same ch-2 sp *(corner)*, *ch 1, (sc in next ch-1 sp, ch 1) across to next corner ch-2 sp, (2 sc, ch 2, 2 sc) in corner ch-2 *sp (corner)*, rep from * twice, ch 1, (sc in next ch-1 sp, ch 1) across to beg sc, join in beg sc. Fasten off. ■

CONNECTICUT WAVED CABLES

Continued from page 137

ASSEMBLY

Referring to assembly diagram for placement, place 2 Panels side by side with WS tog, working through both thicknesses at same time, join embers in top left ch-2 sp, ch 1, working left to right in **reverse sc** *(Fig. 1)*, sc in same sp, *ch 1, sc in next ch-2 sp, rep from * across. Fasten off. Rep for rem Panels.

Connecticut Waved Cables
Assembly Diagram

BORDER

Row 1: Hold piece with RS facing, join chocolate in upper right corner sp, *[hdc in next ch-1 sp, ch 1, sk next sc] across

ends of joined strips, working [hdc, ch 2, hdc, ch 2, hdc] in corner, working down next side, [hdc in next ch-1 sp, ch 1, sk next sc] 7 times, **[hdc dec *(see Stitch Guide)* in next 2 ch-2 sp] 4 times, [hdc in next ch-1 sp, ch 1, sk next sc] 8 times, rep from ** down side, rep from * for rem end and side. Fasten off.

Rnd 2: Join embers in any ch-1 sp, working from left to right, *ch 3, reverse sc in next ch-1 sp, rep from * around, join with sl st in beg reverse sc. Fasten off. ∎

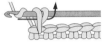

Fig. 1
Reverse Single Crochet

DIAMONDS IN THE SKY

Continued from page 138

3rd ch of beg ch-3. Turn. *(76 dc, 4 ch-3 sps)*
Rnd 6: Ch 5 *(see Pattern Notes)*, sk next 2 dc, dc in next dc, ch 2, sk next 2 dc, dc in each of next 7 dc, *(2 dc, ch 3, 2 dc) in next corner ch-2 sp *(corner)*, dc in each of next 7 dc, ch 2, sk next 2 dc, dc in next dc, ch 2, sk next 2 dc, dc in each of next 7 dc, rep from * twice, (2 dc, ch 3, 2 dc) in next corner ch-2 sp *(corner)*, dc in each of next 6 dc, join in 3rd ch of beg ch-5, sl st in next ch-2 sp. Turn. *(76 dc, 4 ch-3 sps, 8 ch-2 sps)*
Rnd 7: Ch 5, sk first 2 sl sts, sk next dc, dc in each of next 7 dc, *(2 dc, ch 3, 2 dc) in next corner ch-2 sp *(corner)*, dc in each of next 7 dc **, [ch 2, dc in next ch-2 sp] twice, ch 2, sk next 2 dc, dc in each of next 7 dc, rep from * 3 times, ending last rep at **, ch 2, dc in next ch-2 sp, ch 2, join in 3rd ch of beg ch-5. Fasten off. *(80 dc, 4 ch-3 sps, 9 ch-2 sps)*

ASSEMBLY

Join Blocks tog in 7 rows of 5 Blocks each. Sew Blocks tog from 2nd ch of 1 corner to 2nd ch of next corner.

BORDER

Rnd 1: Hold piece with RS facing and 1 short end at top, join yarn with sc in dc before ch-3 sp of upper right-hand corner, *5 sc in next corner ch-3 sp *(corner)*, working across side, sc in each dc, 2 sc in each ch-2 sp, sc in sp before joining, sc in joining, sc in sp after joining, rep from * around, join in beg sc.

Rnd 2: Ch 1, sc in same sc, sk next 2 sc, 6 dc in 3rd sc of next corner, *sk next 2 sc, sc in next sc, sk next 2 sc, 6 sc in next sc, rep from * around, adjusting sts if necessary to have 6 sc in 3rd of each rem corner, join in beg sc. Fasten off. ∎

POODLE AFGHAN
Continued from page 143

Rnd 10: Ch 1, dc in first dc, [picot, dc in next dc] 7 times, * sc in next ch-5 sp, sk next sc, dc in next dc, [picot, dc in next dc] 7 times, rep from * across to next corner, sc in first ch-5 sp, ch 1, [dc, ch 1] twice in each of next 3 ch-1 sps, sc in last ch-5 sp, sk next sc, dc in next dc, [picot, dc in next dc] 7 times, **sc in next ch-5 sp, sk next sc, dc in next dc, [picot, dc in next dc] 7 times, rep from ** across to next corner, sc in first ch-5 sp, ch 1, [dc, ch 1] twice in each of next 3 ch-1 sps, sc in last ch-5 sp, sk next sc, dc in next dc, [picot, dc in next dc] 7 times, *** sc in next ch-5 sp, sk next sc, dc in next dc, [picot, dc in next dc] 7 times, rep from *** across to next corner, sc in first ch-5 sp, ch 1, [dc, ch 1] twice in each of next 3 ch-1 sps, sc in last ch-5 sp, sk next sc, dc in next dc, [picot, dc in next dc] 7 times, **** sc in next ch-5 sp, sk next sc, dc in next dc, [picot, dc in next dc] 7 times, rep from ***** across to next corner, sc in first ch-5 sp, ch 1, [dc, ch 1] twice in each of next 3 ch-1 sps, sc in last ch-5 sp, join in next sp. Fasten off.
Rnds 11–13: With black, rep rnds 8–10. ∎

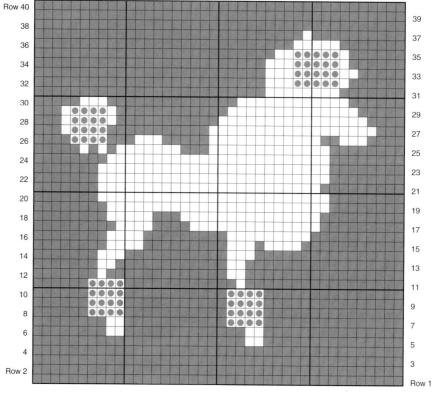

Poodle Afghan
Square

COLOR KEY
■ Plum Wine
□ White/Black
⊙ Placement of puff balls

PINEAPPLES & LACE
Continued from page 144

Row 4: Ch 5, V-st in ch-1 sp of next V-st, ch 2, (2 dc, ch 3, 2 dc) in next ch-3 sp, ch 2, V-st in ch-1 sp of next V-st, turn. *(2 V-sts, 4 dc, 1 ch-5 sp, 1 ch-3 sp, 2 ch-2 sp)*

Row 5: Ch 5, V-st in ch-1 sp of next V-st, ch 2, sk next ch-2 sp, 8 dc in next ch-3 sp, ch 2, V-st in ch-1 sp of next V-st, turn. *(2 V-sts, 8 dc, 1 ch-5 sp, 2 ch-2 sps)*

Row 6: Ch 5, V-st in ch-1 sp of next V-st, ch 3, sk next ch-2 sp, [dc in next dc, ch 1] 7 times, dc in next dc, ch 3, V-st in ch-1 sp of next V-st, turn. *(2 V-sts, 8 dc, 1 ch-5 sp, 2 ch-3 sps, 7 ch-1 sps)*

Row 7: Ch 5, V-st in ch-1 sp of next V-st, sk next ch-3 sp, ch 3, [sc in next ch-1 sp, ch 3] 7 times, V-st in ch-1 sp of next V-st, turn. *(2 V-sts, 7 sc, 1 ch-5 sp, 8 ch-3 sps)*

Row 8: Ch 5, V-st in ch-1 of next V-st, sk next ch-3 sp, *ch 3, sc in next ch-3 sp, rep from * across to last ch-3 sp, sk last ch-3 sp, V-st in ch-1 sp of next V-st, turn.

Rows 9–12: Rep row 8.

Row 13: Ch 5, V-st in ch-1 sp of next V-st, ch 3, sk next ch-3 sp, sc in next ch-3 sp, ch 3, sk next ch-3 sp, V-st in ch-1 sp of next V-st, turn. *(2 V-sts, 1 sc, 1 ch-5 sp, 2 ch-3 sps)*

Row 14: Ch 5, V-st in ch-1 sp of each of next 2 V-sts. Fasten off. *(2 V-sts)*

ASSEMBLY

To join Pineapples to outer edge, lay Body with RS facing and row 1 at bottom.

Step 1: Starting at bottom right corner and working across side, hold first Pineapple with RS of row 1 facing and beg ring at bottom right corner of Body, with top angling up and to right.

Step 2: Tack beg ring of 1 Pineapple to 2nd

st past corner st on Body, running yarn under sts of edge of Body as you work, [sk next 4 sts on Body, tack next ch-5 sp on left edge of Pineapple to next st on Body] 3 times.

Step 3: Sk next 11 sts on Body, tack beg ring of next Pineapple to next st, [sk next 4 sts on Body, tack next ch-5 sp on left edge of Pineapple to next st on Body] 3 times.

Step 4: Rep Step 3 until there are 9 Pineapples across side.

Step 5: Turn corner and tack beg ring of next Pineapple to 2nd st past corner st of Body, [sk 2 sts on Body, tack next ch-5 sp on left edge of Pineapple to next st on Body] 3 times.

Step 6: Sk next 8 sts on Body, tack beg ring of next Pineapple to next st, [sk next 2 sts on Body, tack next ch-5 sp on left edge of Pineapple to next st on Body] 3 times.

Step 7: Rep Step 6 until there are 6 Pineapples across end.

Step 8: Rep Steps 2–7 to tack 9 Pineapples across rem side and 6 Pineapples across rem end of Body.

Step 9: Lay Afghan on floor or bed, smoothing Pineapples out flat.

Step 10: Tack ch-5 sps on rows 10 and 12 at left edge of 1 Pineapple to ch-5 sps on rows 3 and 5 at right edge of next Pineapple.

Step 11: Rep Step 11 across to next corner.

Step 12: To join corner Pineapples, tack next 2 ch-5 sps on rows at left edge of last Pineapple to beg ring and ch-5 sp of row 3 on next Pineapple around corner.

Step 13: Rep Steps 10–12 until all Pineapples are joined to Body. ∎

Forever Quilts

Our rendition of quilt pattern afghans is sure to take you back to those cold winter nights when you were snuggled under a handmade quilt. Pass the memories on with this beautiful selection of quilt-look afghans.

Eight-Pointed Star Afghan

Design by Glenda Winkleman

SKILL LEVEL
 INTERMEDIATE

FINISHED SIZE
42 x 60 inches

MATERIALS
- TLC Essentials medium (worsted) weight yarn (6 oz/312 yds/ 170g per skein):
    6 skeins #2316 winter white
    2 skeins each #2220 butter and #2883 country blue
- Size K/10½/6.5mm afghan hook or size needed to obtain gauge
- Size I/9/5.5mm regular crochet hook
- Tapestry needle

GAUGE
15 afghan sts = 4 inches; 13 afghan st rows = 4 inches
Block = 8 x 9¾ inches

PATTERN NOTES
Weave in ends as work progresses.

Join with a slip stitch unless otherwise stated.

For afghan stitch color change, drop current color, insert hook under next vertical bar, yarn over with next color, draw loop through; to work stitches off hook, *work until 1 loop of current color remains on hook, drop current color, pick up next color from under first color, yarn over, draw through 2 loops on hook, rep from * across.

Do not carry yarn across back of work for more than 2 or 3 stitches, use new bobbin for each section of color. Always pick up next color from under current color to prevent a gap from forming.

Fasten off colors at the end of each color section.

Chain-3 at beginning of double crochet rounds count as first double crochet unless otherwise stated.

INSTRUCTIONS

BLOCK
Make 12.
Row 1: With afghan hook and winter white, ch 31, insert hook in 2nd ch from hook, yo, draw lp through, *insert hook in next ch, yo, draw lp through, rep from * across, **do not turn, to work lps off hook,** yo, draw lp through 1 lp on hook *(Fig. 1)*, **yo, draw lp through 2 lps on hook, rep from ** across until 1 lp on hook *(Fig. 2)*, **do not turn.**
Row 2: Sk first vertical bar, *insert hook under next vertical bar *(Fig. 3)*,

Fig. 1

Fig. 2

Fig. 3

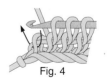
Fig. 4

Eight-Pointed Star
Afghan Stitch Illustration

Continued on page 168

Log Cabin

Design by Delma Myers

SKILL LEVEL

■■□□ EASY

FINISHED SIZE
53 x 72½ inches

MATERIALS
• Lion Brand Vanna's Choice medium (worsted) weight yarn (3½ oz/170 yds/100g per ball):
    5 balls #108 dusty
    4 balls each #105 silver blue and #143 antique rose
    3 balls each #099 linen and #140 dusty rose
    2 balls each #173 dusty green and #174 olive
• Sizes G/6/4mm and H/8/5mm crochet hooks or size needed to obtain gauge
• Tapestry needle

GAUGE
With size H hook: 13 sts = 4 inches

PATTERN NOTES
Weave in ends as work progresses.

Join with a slip stitch unless otherwise stated.

Chain-3 at beginning of double crochet rounds counts as first double crochet unless otherwise stated.

INSTRUCTIONS

SQUARE
Make 48.
First Section
Row 1 (RS): With size H hook and linen, ch 7, sc in 2nd ch from hook, sc in each rem ch, turn. *(6 sc)*
Row 2: Ch 1, sc in each sc across, turn.
Rows 3–5: Rep row 2.
Row 6: Ch 1, sc in each sc across. Fasten off.

2nd Section
Row 1: Join dusty green in side of last sc of row 6, sc in end of each of next 5 rows, working across next side in unused lps of beg ch, 3 sc in first lp *(corner)*, sc in each of next 5 lps, turn. *(13 sc)*
Row 2: Ch 1, sc in each sc to 2nd sc of next corner, 3 sc in 2nd sc *(corner)*, sc in each rem sc across, turn. *(15 sc)*
Row 3: Rep row 2. *(17 sc)*
Row 4: Ch 1, sc in each sc to 2nd sc of next corner, 3 sc in 2nd sc *(corner)*, sc in each rem sc across. Fasten off. *(19 sc)*

3rd Section
Row 1: Join olive in side of last sc of row 4 of previous section, sc in end of each row or in each sc to next corner, working across next side, 3 sc in next st *(corner)*, sc in each sc or in end of each row across, turn. *(21 sc)*
Row 2: Ch 1, sc in each sc to 2nd sc of next corner, 3 sc in 2nd sc *(corner)*, sc in each sc across, turn. *(23 sc)*
Row 3: Rep row 2. *(25 sc)*

Continued on page 170

Garden Cat Afghan

Design by Martha Brooks Stein

SKILL LEVEL

 INTERMEDIATE

FINISHED SIZE

49 x 65 inches

MATERIALS

- Medium (worsted) weight yarn:
  22½ oz/1,125 yds/641g
  dark green
  18 oz/900 yds/109g white
  5 oz/250 yds/42g black
  1½ oz/75 yds/42g dark red
  1 oz/50 yds/28g each medium red,
  red and medium green
  ½ oz/25 yds/14g each teal, orange,
  dark yellow, bright red, purple, yellow,
  violet, medium pink, dark pink, gold,
  light purple, dark rose and dark orange
- Size I/9/5.5mm crochet hook or size
  needed to obtain gauge
- Tapestry needle

GAUGE

Square = 2¾ inches

PATTERN NOTES

Weave in ends as work progresses.

Join with a slip stitch unless otherwise stated.

Chain-3 at beginning of double crochet
rounds counts as first double crochet unless
otherwise stated.

INSTRUCTIONS

SOLID SQUARE

Make 152 dark green; 85 white; 33 black; 8
dark red; 6 medium red; 4 red; 2 each dark
pink and medium pink; and 1 each dark
rose, light purple, gold, dark yellow, orange,
purple, violet and bright red.

Rnd 1 (RS): Ch 4, join in first ch to form a
ring, **ch 3** *(see Pattern Notes)*, 2 dc in ring, ch
2, [3 dc in ring, ch 2] 3 times, join in 3rd ch
of beg ch-3. *(12 dc, 4 ch sps)*

Rnd 2: Sl st in each of next 2 sts, sl st in next
ch-2 sp, ch 3, (2 dc, ch 2, 3 dc) in same sp, ch
1, [(3 dc, ch 2, 3 dc) in next ch-2 sp, ch 1] 3
times, join in 3rd ch of beg ch-3. Fasten off.
(24 dc, 4 ch sps, 8 ch-1 sps)

HALF-COLOR

Make 16 white/medium green; 10 white/dark
red; 8 white/medium red; 7 white/black; 6
white/dark yellow; 4 each red/black, white/
gold, white/teal and white/yellow; 2 each
white/red, white/dark rose, white/purple,
white/violet, white/medium pink, white/dark
pink, white/orange, white/light purple and
white/bright red.

Rnd 1 (RS): With first color, ch 4, join in
first ch to form a ring, ch 3, sl st in 2nd ch
from hook *(joining lp)*, (2 dc, ch 2, 3 dc) in
ring, ch 1 **changing color** *(see Stitch Guide)*
to next color, ch 1, (3 dc, ch 2, 3 dc) in ring,
ch 1, join in joining lp. Fasten off both colors.
(12 dc, 4 ch sps)

Continued on page 171

Little Denim Jeans

Design by Frances Hughes

SKILL LEVEL

■■■□ INTERMEDIATE

FINISHED SIZE

43 x 64 inches

MATERIALS

- Medium (worsted) weight yarn:
  25 oz/1,250 yds/708g navy
  21 oz/105 yds/594g off-white
  8½ oz/425 yds/241g each blue and tan
  4 oz/200 yds/113g each brown and variegated

  4 MEDIUM
- Size G/6/4mm afghan hook or size needed to obtain gauge
- Size G/6/4mm crochet hook
- Tapestry needle

GAUGE

With afghan hook: 5 sts = 1 inch; 16 afghan st rows = 4 inches

PATTERN NOTES

Weave in ends as work progresses.

Join with a slip stitch unless otherwise stated.

For afghan stitch color change, drop current color, insert hook under next vertical bar, yarn over with next color, draw loop through; to work stitches off hook, work until 1 loop of current color remains on hook, drop current color, pick up next color from under first color, yarn over, draw through 2 loops on hook.

Do not carry yarn across back of work for more than 2 or 3 stitches, use new bobbin for each section of color. Always pick up next color from under current color to prevent a gap from forming.

Fasten off colors at the end of each color section.

INSTRUCTIONS

Row 1 (RS): With afghan hook and navy, ch 210, insert hook in 2nd ch from hook, yo, draw lp through, *insert hook in next ch, yo, draw lp through, rep from * across, **do not turn,** to work **lps off hook,** yo, draw through 1 lp on hook *(Fig. 1),* **yo, draw through 2 lps on hook, rep from ** across until 1 lp on hook *(Fig. 2),* **do not turn.** *(210 sts)*

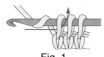
Fig. 1

Fig. 2

Row 2: Sk first vertical bar, *insert hook **under next vertical bar** *(Fig. 3),* yo, draw lp through, rep from * across to last vertical bar; **insert hook under last bar and st directly behind it** *(Fig. 4),* yo, draw lp through, work sts off hook.

Fig. 3

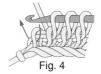
Fig. 4

Rows 3–8: Rep row 2.
Row 9: Sk first vertical bar, [insert hook under

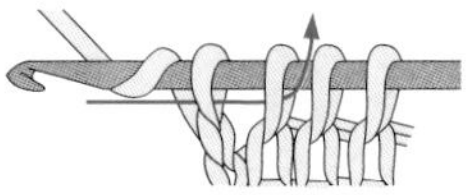

Little Denim Jeans
Afghan Stitch Illustration

next vertical bar, yo, draw lp through] 12 times, *change color *(see Pattern Notes)* to off-white, [insert hook under next vertical bar, yo, draw lp through] 54 times, change color to navy, [insert hook under next vertical bar, yo, draw lp through] 12 times, rep from * once, change color to off-white, [insert hook under next vertical bar, yo, draw lp through] 54 times, change color to navy, [insert hook under next vertical bar, yo, draw lp through] 11 times, insert hook under last bar and st directly behind it, yo, draw lp through, work sts off hook **changing colors** *(see Pattern Notes)* as needed.

Rows 10–12: Rep row 9.

Row 13: Sk first vertical bar, [insert hook under next vertical bar, yo, draw lp through] 12 times, *change color to off-white, [insert hook under next vertical bar, yo, draw lp through] 16 times, change color to brown, [insert hook under next vertical bar, yo, draw lp through] 6 times, change color to off-white, [insert hook under next vertical bar, yo, draw lp through] 10 times, change color to brown, [insert hook under next vertical bar, yo, draw lp through] 6 times, change color to off-white, [insert hook under next vertical bar, yo, draw lp through] 16 times, change color to navy, [insert hook under next vertical bar, yo, draw lp through] 12 times, rep from * once, change color to off-white, [insert hook under next vertical bar, yo, draw lp through] 16 times, change color to brown, [insert hook under next vertical bar, yo, draw lp through] 6 times, change color to off-white, [insert hook under next vertical bar, yo, draw lp through] 10 times, change color to brown, [insert hook under next vertical bar, yo, draw lp through] 6 times, change color to off-white, [insert hook under next vertical

bar, yo, draw lp through] 16 times, change color to navy, [insert hook under next vertical bar, yo, draw lp through] 11 times, insert hook under last bar and st directly behind it, yo, draw lp through, work sts off hook.

Row 14: Sk first vertical bar, *[insert hook under next vertical bar, yo, draw lp through] 12 times, work according to chart, change color to navy, [insert hook under next vertical bar, yo, draw lp through] 12 times, rep from * once, [insert hook under next vertical bar, yo, draw lp through] 12 times, work according to chart, change color to navy, [insert hook under next vertical bar, yo, draw lp through] 11 times, insert hook under last bar and st directly behind it, yo, draw lp through; work sts off hook.

Rows 15–76: Rep row 14.

Rows 77–84: With navy, rep row 2.

Rows 85–236: [Rep rows 9–84 consecutively] twice.

EDGING

Rnd 1 (RS): With size G crochet hook, ch 1, sc in each st and in end of each row around and work 3 sc in each corner, join in first sc.

Rnd 2: Ch 1, working left to right, work **reverse sc** *(see Fig. 5)* in each sc around, join in beg reverse sc. Fasten off. ∎

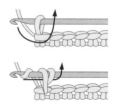

Fig. 5
Reverse Single Crochet

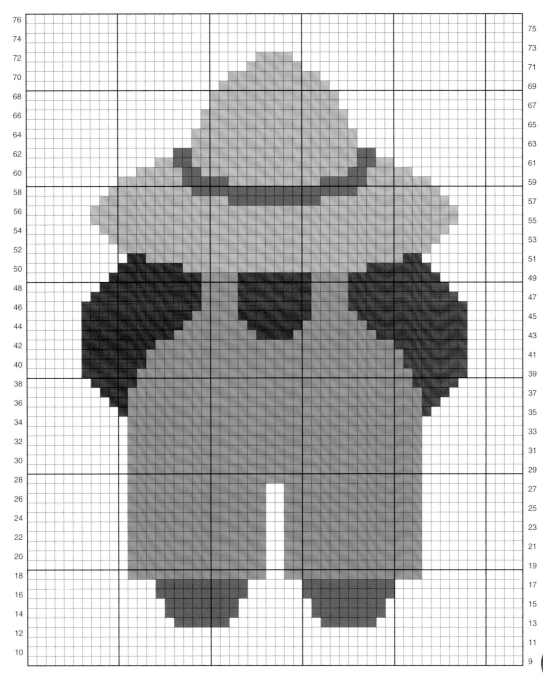

Little Denim Jeans
Chart

COLOR KEY
☐ Off-white
▨ Navy
▨ Tan
▨ Brown
■ Variegated

Granny's Garden

Design by Glenda Winkleman

SKILL LEVEL

 INTERMEDIATE

FINISHED SIZE

42 x 64 inches

MATERIALS

- TLC Essentials medium (worsted)
  weight yarn (6 oz/312 yds/170g
  per skein):
    4 skeins each #2316 winter white
    and #2673 medium thyme
    1 skein each #2672 light thyme, #2220
    butter, #2772 light country rose, #2883
    country blue and #2531 light plum
- Size I/9/5.5mm crochet hook or size
  needed to obtain gauge
- Tapestry needle

GAUGE

Square = 6½ inches

PATTERN NOTES

Weave in ends as work progresses.

Join with a slip stitch unless otherwise stated.

Chain-3 at beginning of double crochet
rounds counts as first double crochet unless
otherwise stated.

Chain-4 at beginning of treble crochet
rounds counts as first treble crochet unless
otherwise stated.

SPECIAL STITCHES

Popcorn (pc): 3 dc in indicated st, remove
hook, insert hook from front to back in first
dc, insert hook through previously dropped
lp, yo, draw lp through 2 lps on hook.
Picot: Ch 3, sl st in indicated st.

INSTRUCTIONS

SQUARE

Make 54.

*Note: Rnds 1 and 2 do not specify exact colors; use
butter, light country rose, country blue and light
plum as desired.*

Rnd 1 (RS): With desired color, ch 5,
join in first ch to form ring, [sc in ring, ch 2]
8 times, **join** in beg sc. Fasten off. *(8 sc,
8 ch-2 sps)*

Rnd 2: Join 2nd color in any ch-2 sp, (pc—*see
Special Stitches*, ch 3, pc) same sp as joining,
ch 3, [(pc, ch 3, pc) in next ch-2 sp, ch 3]
7 times, join in top of beg pc. Fasten off.
(16 pc, 16 ch-3 sps)

Rnd 3: Join light thyme in first ch-3 sp of
previous rnd, **ch 3** *(see Pattern Notes)*, (dc, ch
2, 2 dc) in same sp *(beg corner)*, ch 6, *sk next
3 ch-3 sps, (2 dc, ch 2, 2 dc) in next ch-3 sp
(corner), ch 6, rep from * twice, join in 3rd ch
of beg ch-3. Fasten off.

Rnd 4: Join winter white in ch-2 sp of beg
corner of previous rnd, **ch 4** *(see Pattern
Notes)*, (2 tr, ch 2, 3 tr) in same sp *(beg
corner)*, 2 tr in each of next 3 ch-3 sps on rnd
2, *(3 tr, ch 2, 3 tr) in next corner ch-2 sp
(corner), 2 tr in each of next 3 ch-3 sps on rnd
2, rep from * twice, join in 4th ch of beg ch-4.

Rnd 5: Ch 3, dc in each of next 2 tr, (2 dc, ch 2, 2 dc) in next corner ch-2 sp *(corner)*, *dc in each of next 12 tr, (2 dc, ch 2, 2 dc) in next corner ch-2 sp *(corner)*, rep from * twice, dc in each of next 9 tr, join in 3rd ch of beg ch-3. Fasten off.

Rnd 6: Join medium thyme in any corner ch-2 sp, ch 3, (2 dc, ch 2, 3 dc) in same sp *(beg corner)*, [sk next 2 dc, 2 dc in sp between last sk dc and next dc] 7 times, sk next 2 dc, *(3 dc, ch 2, 3 dc) in next corner ch-2 sp *(corner)*, [sk next 2 dc, 2 dc in sp between sk dc and next dc] 7 times, sk next 2 dc, rep from * twice, join in 3rd ch of beg ch-3. Fasten off.

ASSEMBLY
Arrange Squares as desired in 9 rows of 6 Squares each. With tapestry needle and medium thyme, sew squares tog on WS through **back lps** *(see Stitch Guide)*.

BORDER
Note: Ch-2 sp on each side of square joinings count as a st.

Hold piece with RS facing, join medium thyme in any corner ch-2 sp, ch 3, (2 dc, ch 2, 3 dc) in same sp, *dc in each of next 2 sts, **picot** *(see Special Stitches)* in last st, rep from * across to next corner ch-2 sp, (3 dc, ch 2, 3 dc) in corner ch-2 sp, **dc in each of next 2 sts, picot in last st, rep from ** across to next corner ch-2 sp, (3 dc, ch 2, 3 dc) in corner ch-2 sp, ***dc in each of next 2 sts, picot in last st, rep from *** across to next corner ch-2 sp, (3 dc, ch 2, 3 dc) in corner ch-2 sp, ****dc in each of next 2 sts, picot in last st, rep from **** across to beg ch-3, join in 3rd ch of beg ch-3. Fasten off. ■

EIGHT-POINTED STAR AFGHAN
Continued from page 156

yo, draw lp through, rep from * across to last st, **insert hook under last bar and st directly behind it** *(Fig 4, page 156)*, to work lps off hook, yo, draw lp through 1 lp on hook, **yo, draw lp through 2 lps on hook, rep from ** across until 1 lp on hook.

Row 3: Rep row 2.

Rows 4–31: Following chart, rep row 2, **changing colors** *(see Pattern Notes)* as indicated on chart.

Row 32: Sl st in each vertical bar across. Fasten off.

Border
Rnd 1 (RS): Hold Block with RS facing, with size I crochet hook, join winter white in first st in upper right-hand corner, ch 1, sc in each of first 4 sts, [**sc dec** *(see Stitch Guide)* in next 2 sts, sc in each of next 3 sts] 5 times, sc in next st, ch 2 *(corner)*, working across next side in ends of rows, sc in each row to next corner, ch 2 *(corner)*, working across next side in unused lps of beg ch, sc in each

of next 4 sts, [sc dec in next 2 sts, sc in each of next 3 sts] 5 times, sc in next st, ch 2 *(corner)*, working across next side in ends of rows, sc in each row to next corner, ch 2 *(corner)*, join in beg sc.

Rnd 2: Ch 1, *hdc in each sc to next corner ch-2 sp, (2 hdc, ch 2, 2 hdc) in corner ch-2 sp *(corner)*, rep from * 3 times, join in beg hdc. Fasten off.

Note: On following rnd, hold 1 strand of butter and and 1 strand of country blue tog. Using strands separately and beg with country blue, alternate colors for each st.

Rnd 3: Join strands with sl st in any corner ch-2 sp, **ch 3** *(see Pattern Notes)*, (dc, ch 2, 2 dc) in same sp *(beg corner)*, sk next hdc, dc in each hdc to next corner ch-2 sp, *(2 dc, ch 2, 2 dc) in corner ch-2 sp *(corner)*, sk next hdc, dc in each hdc across to next corner ch-2 sp, rep from * twice, join in 3rd ch of beg ch-3. Fasten off.

Rnd 4: Join winter white in any corner ch-2 sp, ch 1, (hdc, ch 2, hdc) in same sp *(corner)*, *hdc in each dc to next corner ch-2 sp, (hdc, ch 2, hdc) in corner ch-2 sp *(corner)*, rep from * twice, hdc in each dc to beg hdc, join in beg hdc.

Rnd 5: Ch 1, hdc in same hdc, (2 hdc, ch 2, 2 hdc) in next ch-2 sp *(corner)*, *hdc in each hdc to next corner ch-2 sp, (2 hdc, ch 2, 2 hdc) in corner ch-2 sp *(corner)*, rep from * twice, hdc in each hdc to beg hdc, join in beg hdc. Fasten off.

ASSEMBLY

Join Blocks in 4 rows of 3 Blocks each. With winter white and working in **back lps** *(see Stitch Guide)* only, sl st Blocks tog.

BORDER

Rnd 1 (RS): Hold piece with RS facing and 1 short end at top, join winter white in ch-2 sp in right-hand corner, ch 3, (dc, ch 2, 2 dc) in same sp *(beg corner)*, *sk next hdc, dc in each hdc and in each ch sp on each side of joinings across to next corner ch-2 sp, (2 dc, ch 2, 2 dc) in corner ch-2 sp *(corner)*, rep from *

twice, sk next hdc, dc in each hdc and in each ch sp on each side of joinings across to beg ch-3, join in 3rd ch of beg ch-3.

Rnd 2: Ch 1, hdc in same ch as joining, hdc in next dc, (hdc, ch 2, hdc) in next ch-2 sp *(corner)*, *hdc in each dc to next corner ch-2 sp, (hdc, ch 2, hdc) in corner ch-2 sp *(corner)*, rep from * twice, hdc in each hdc to beg hdc, join in beg hdc. Fasten off.

Rnd 3: Join butter in same hdc as joining, ch 3, *dc in each hdc to next corner ch-2 sp, 8 dc in corner ch-2 sp *(corner)*, rep from * 3 times, dc in each hdc to beg ch-3, join in 3rd ch of beg ch-3.

Rnd 4: Ch 3, dc in each of next 2 dc, *[2 dc in next dc, dc in next dc] 4 times, dc in each dc across to first dc of next 7-dc corner, rep from * twice, [2 dc in next dc, dc in next dc] 4 times, dc in each dc across to beg ch-3, join in 3rd ch of beg ch-3. Fasten off.

Rnd 5: Join country blue in same ch as joining, ch 3, dc in next dc, ch 3, sl st in last dc, *dc in each of next 2 dc, ch 3, sl st in last dc made, rep from * around to last dc, dc in last dc, join in 3rd ch of beg ch-3. Fasten off. ■

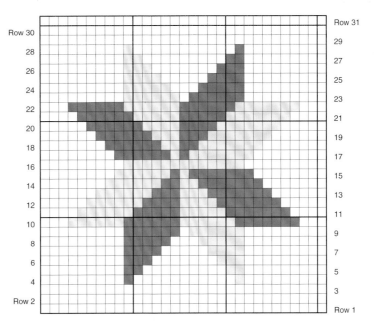

COLOR KEY
☐ Butter
■ Country Blue
☐ White

Eight-Pointed Star Afghan
Chart

LOG CABIN
Continued from page 159

Continued from page 159

Row 4: Ch 1, sc in each sc to 2nd sc of next corner, 3 sc in 2nd sc *(corner)*, sc in each sc across. Fasten off. *(27 sc)*

4th Section
Row 1: Join dusty rose in side of last sc of row 4 of previous section, sc in end of each row or in each sc to next corner, working across next side, 3 sc in next st *(corner)*, sc in each sc or in end of each row across, turn. *(29 sc)*
Row 2: Ch 1, sc in each sc to 2nd sc of next corner, 3 sc in 2nd sc *(corner)*, sc in each sc across, turn. *(31 sc)*
Row 3: Rep row 2. *(33 sc)*
Row 4: Ch 1, sc in each sc to 2nd sc of next corner, 3 sc in 2nd sc *(corner)*, sc in each sc across. Fasten off. *(35 sc)*

5th Section
Row 1: Join antique rose in side of last sc of row 4 of previous section, sc in end of each row or in each sc to 2nd sc of next corner, 3 sc in 2nd sc *(corner)*, sc in each sc or in end of each row to end, turn. *(37 sc)*
Row 2: Ch 1, sc in each sc to 2nd sc of next corner, 3 sc in 2nd sc *(corner)*, sc in each sc across, turn. *(39 sc)*
Row 3: Rep row 2. *(41 sc)*
Row 4: Ch 1, sc in each sc to 2nd sc of next corner, 3 sc in 2nd sc *(corner)*, sc in each sc across. Fasten off. *(43 sc)*

6th Section
Row 1: Join silver blue in side of last sc of row 4 of previous section, sc in end of each row or in each sc to 2nd sc of next corner, 3 sc in 2nd sc *(corner)*, sc in each sc or in end of each row to end, turn. *(45 sc)*
Row 2: Ch 1, sc in each sc to 2nd sc of next corner, 3 sc in 2nd sc *(corner)*, sc in each sc across, turn. *(47 sc)*
Row 3: Rep row 2. *(49 sc)*
Row 4: Ch 1, sc in each sc to 2nd sc of next corner, 3 sc in 2nd sc *(corner)*, sc in each sc across. Fasten off. *(51 sc)*

7th Section
Row 1: Join dusty in side of last sc of row 4, sc in end of each row or in each sc to 2nd sc of next corner, 3 sc in 2nd sc

(corner), sc in each sc or in end of each row to end, turn. *(53 sc)*
Row 2: Ch 1, sc in each sc to 2nd sc of next corner, 3 sc in 2nd sc *(corner)*, sc in each sc across, turn. *(55 sc)*
Row 3: Rep row 2. *(57 sc)*
Row 4: Ch 1, sc in each sc to 2nd sc of next corner, 3 sc in 2nd sc *(corner)*, sc in each sc across. Fasten off. *(59 sc)*

ASSEMBLY
Referring to assembly diagram, sew Squares tog in 8 rows of 6 Squares each with matching yarn colors.

Log Cabin
Assembly Diagram

EDGING
Rnd 1 (RS): Hold piece with RS facing and 1 short end at top, with size H hook, join linen in 2nd sc of upper right-hand corner, 2 sc in same sc *(beg corner)*, *sc in each sc to 2nd sc of next corner, 3 sc in 2nd sc *(corner)*, rep from *

twice, sc in each sc to beg sc, sc in same sc as beg sc, join in beg sc. Fasten off. Turn.

Rnd 2: Join linen in 2nd sc of different corner, 2 sc in same sc *(beg corner)*, *sc in each sc to 2nd sc of next corner, 3 sc in 2nd sc *(corner)*, rep from * twice, sc in each sc to beg sc, sc in same sc as beg sc, join in beg sc. Fasten off. Turn.

Rnds 3–5: Rep rnd 2. At end of last rnd, do not fasten off.

Rnd 6: With size G hook, ch 1, working left

to right, work **reverse sc** *(see Fig. 1)* in each sc around, join in beg reverse sc. Fasten off. ■

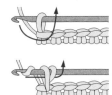

Fig. 1
Reverse Single Crochet

GARDEN CAT AFGHAN

Continued from page 160

Rnd 2: Join first color in last ch sp made, ch 3, sl st in 2nd ch from hook *(joining lp)*, 2 dc in same sp, ch 1, (3 dc, ch 2, 3 dc) in next ch sp, ch 1, 3 dc in next ch sp, ch 1 changing color to next color, ch 1, 3 dc in same sp, ch 1, (3 dc, ch 2, 3 dc) in last ch sp, ch 1, 3 dc in same ch sp as first 3 dc, ch 1, join in joining lp. Fasten off both colors.

THREE-FOURTH SQUARE

Make 2 each white/medium pink, white/dark red and white/dark pink.

Rnd 1 (RS): With first color, ch 4, join in first ch to form a ring, ch 3, sl st in 2nd ch from hook *(joining lp)*, (2 dc, ch 2, 3 dc, ch 2, 3 dc) in ring, ch 1 changing color to next color, ch 1, 3 dc in ring, ch 1, join in joining lp. Fasten off both colors. *(12 dc, 4 ch sps)*

Rnd 2: Join first color in last ch sp made, ch 3, sl st in 2nd ch from hook *(joining lp)*, 2 dc in same sp, [ch 1, (3 dc, ch 2, 3 dc) in next 2 ch sp] twice, ch 1, 3 dc in last ch sp, ch 1 changing color to next color, ch 1, 3 dc in same sp, ch 1, 3 dc in same ch sp as first 3 dc, ch 1, join in joining lp. Fasten off both colors.

THREE-COLOR SQUARE

Make 4 white/black/dark orange.

Rnd 1 (RS): With white, ch 4, join in first ch to form a ring, ch 3, sl st in 2nd ch from hook *(joining lp)*, (2 dc, ch 2, 3 dc) in ring, ch 1 changing color to black, ch 1, (3 dc, ch 2,

3 dc) in ring, ch 1, join in joining lp. Fasten off both colors. *(12 dc, 4 ch sps)*

Rnd 2: Join white in last ch sp made, ch 3, sl st in 2nd ch from hook *(joining lp)*, 2 dc in same sp, ch 1, (3 dc, ch 2, 3 dc) in next ch sp, ch 1, 3 dc in next ch sp, ch 1 changing color to dark orange, ch 1, 3 dc in same sp, ch 1, (3 dc, ch 2, 3 dc) in last ch sp, ch 1, 3 dc in same ch sp as first 3 dc, ch 1, join in joining lp. Fasten off both colors.

ASSEMBLY

Referring to assembly diagram, sew Squares tog through **back lps** *(see Stitch Guide)* with matching yarn colors.

FINISHING

Referring to assembly diagram for placement, with black and using **split stitch** *(Fig. 1)*, embroider antennae on butterflies.

Fig. 1
Garden Cat Afghan
Split Stitch

BORDER

Rnd 1 (RS): Hold piece with RS facing and 1 short end at top, working in back lps only, join dark green with sc in first ch of upper right-hand corner sp, ch 2 *(corner)*, sc in next ch of same corner sp *(beg corner)*, work 151

sc evenly spaced across to next corner ch sp, sc in next ch, ch 2 *(corner)*, sc in next ch of same corner sp, working across next side, work 205 sc evenly spaced across to next corner sp, sc in next ch, ch 2 *(corner)*, sc in next ch of same corner sp, working across next side, work 151 sc evenly spaced across to next corner ch sp, sc in next ch, ch 2 *(corner)*, sc in next ch of same corner sp, working across next side, work 205 sc evenly spaced across to joining sc, join in joining sc. *(720 sc, 4 ch-1 sps)*

Rnd 2: Ch 1, (sc, ch 2, sc) in next ch-2 sp *(corner)*, ch 1, sk next sc, *sc in next sc, ch 1, sk next sc, rep from * across to next corner ch-2 sp, (sc, ch 2, sc) in corner ch-2 sp *(corner)*, ch 1, sk next sc, **sc in next sc, ch 1, sk next sc, rep from ** across to next corner ch sp, (sc, ch 2, sc) in corner ch-2 sp *(corner)*, ch 1, sk next sc, ***sc in next sc, ch 1, sk next sc, rep from *** across to next corner ch sp, (sc, ch 2, sc) in corner ch-2 sp *(corner)*, ch 1, sk next sc, ****sc in next sc, ch 1, sk next sc, rep from **** across to beg sc, join in beg sc. Fasten off.

Rnd 3: Join white in first corner ch-2 sp, ch 3, sl st in same sp, ch 3, *sl st in next ch-1 sp, ch 3, rep from * across to next corner ch-2 sp, (sl st, ch 3, sl st) in corner ch-2 sp, ch 3, **sl st in next ch-1 sp, ch 3, rep from ** across to next corner ch-2 sp (sl st, ch 3, sl st) in corner ch-2 sp, ch 3, ***sl st in next ch-1 sp, ch 3, rep from *** across to next corner ch-2 sp, (sl st, ch 3, sl st) in corner ch-2 sp, ch 3, ****sl st in next ch-1 sp, ch 3, rep from ** across to beg sl st, join in beg sl st. Fasten off. ■

Garden Cat Afghan
Assembly Diagram

COLOR & STITCH KEY
- Dark green
- Black
- Dark red
- Medium red
- Bright Red
- Red
- Teal
- Dark yellow
- Orange
- Purple
- Yellow
- White
- Medium green
- Violet
- Dark pink
- Medium pink
- Gold
- Light purple
- Dark rose
- Dark orange
- Split stitch

Special Thanks

We would like to thank the talented crochet designers whose work is featured in this collection.

Cynthia Adams
Jewel Tones Tunisian 50

Renee' Barnes
Ring Around the Rosie
  Baby Afghan 100

Ramona B. Chebli
Old MacDonald's
  Farm 109

Rhonda Dodds
Pearls & Lace 8

Bettie Dowler
Pineapples & Lace 144

JoHanna Dzikowski
Pineapple Connection 76

Holly Fields
Poodle Afghan 141

Norma Gale
Heritage Filet 79
Treasures of the Deep 53

Laura Gebhardt
Frosty Lace 33

Kim Guzman
Buttercream Afghan 112

Anne Halliday
Lacy Cross-Stitch 37
Lacy Squares
  With Scallop Edging 38

Frances Hughes
Little Denim Jeans 163

Rosalie Johnston
Amanda Whorl 11

Patricia Kristofferson
Jeweled Octagons 62

Lucille LaFlamme
Aran Afghan 30
Vintage Florals 41

Peggy Longshore
Shells Filet 80

Melody MacDuffee
Victorian Lace 22

Ruthie Marks
Tree Blossoms 17

Maria Merlino
Double Happiness 92

Christine Moody
Rose Diamond 86

Delma Myers
Diagonal Jewels 66
Log Cabin 159

Joyce Nordstrom
Black Pineapples 89
Connecticut Waved
  Cables 135

Lisa Pflug
Pink Flowers
  Crib Cover 103
Royal Ripples 57

Dorotha Shappie
Pineapples & Lace 144

Darla Sims
Christening Blanket 106
Kaleidoscope Afghan 61

Martha Brooks Stein
Garden Cat 160
Scraps Spectacular 54

Judy Teague Treece
Blue Ice 132
Delicate Pinapples 85

Leshia Tweddle
Rings & Things Afghan 58

Christine Walter
French Stripes 34
Lime Lace 14

Dorothy Warrell
Diamonds in the Sky 138

Glenda Winkleman
Eight-Pointed Star
  Afghan 156
Granny's Garden 166

Lori Zeller
Floral Fantasy 147
Serene Meadow 18

Standard Yarn Weight System

Categories of yarn, gauge ranges, and recommended needle and hook sizes

Yarn Weight Symbol & Category Names	1 SUPER FINE	2 FINE	3 LIGHT	4 MEDIUM	5 BULKY	6 SUPER BULKY
Type of Yarns in Category	Sock, Fingering, Baby	Sport, Baby	DK, Light Worsted	Worsted, Afghan, Aran	Chunky, Craft, Rug	Bulky, Roving
Crochet Gauge* Ranges in Single Crochet to 4 inch	21–32 sts	16–20 sts	12–17 sts	11–14 sts	8–11 sts	5–9 sts
Recommended Hook in Metric Size Range	2.25–3.5 mm	3.5–4.5 mm	4.5–5.5 mm	5.5–6.5 mm	6.5–9 mm	9 mm and larger
Recommended Hook U.S. Size Range	B1–E4	E4–7	7–I-9	I-9–K-10½	K-10½–M-13	M-13 and larger

* GUIDELINES ONLY: The above reflect the most commonly used gauges and hook sizes for specific yarn categories.

Skill Levels

BEGINNER
Beginner projects for first-time crocheters using basic stitches. Minimal shaping.

EASY
Easy projects using basic stitches, repetitive stitch patterns, simple color changes and simple shaping and finishing.

INTERMEDIATE
Intermediate projects with a variety of stitches, mid-level shaping and finishing.

EXPERIENCED
Experienced projects using advanced techniques and stitches, detailed shaping and refined finishing.

Symbols

* An asterisk is used to mark the beginning of a portion of instructions to be worked more than once; thus, "rep from * twice more" means after working the instructions once, repeat the instructions following the asterisk twice more (3 times in all).

( ) Parentheses are used to set off and clarify a group of stitches that are to be worked all into the same space or stitch, such as "in next corner sp work (2 dc, ch 1, 2 dc)."

[ ] Brackets are used to enclose instructions that should be worked the exact number of times specified immediately following the brackets, such as "[2 sc in next dc, sc in next dc] twice."

[ ] Brackets and ( ) parentheses are used to provide additional information to clarify instructions.

Stitch Guide

Abbreviations

beg	begin/beginning
bpdc	back post double crochet
bpsc	back post single crochet
bptr	back post treble crochet
CC	contrasting color
ch	chain stitch
ch-	refers to chain or space previously made (e.g., ch-1 space)
ch sp	chain space
cl	cluster
cm	centimeter(s)
dc	double crochet
dec	decrease/decreases/decreasing
dtr	double treble crochet
fpdc	front post double crochet
fpsc	front post single crochet
fptr	front post treble crochet
g	gram(s)
hdc	half double crochet
inc	increase/increases/increasing
lp(s)	loop(s)
MC	main color
mm	millimeter(s)
oz	ounce(s)
pc	popcorn
rem	remain/remaining
rep	repeat(s)
rnd(s)	round(s)
RS	right side
sc	single crochet
sk	skip(ped)
sl st	slip stitch
sp(s)	space(s)
st(s)	stitch(es)
tog	together
tr	treble crochet
trtr	triple treble crochet
WS	wrong side
yd(s)	yard(s)
yo	yarn over

Chain—ch: Yo, pull through lp on hook.

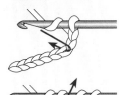

Slip stitch—sl st: Insert hook in st, pull through both lps on hook.

Single crochet—sc: Insert hook in st, yo, pull through st, yo, pull through both lps on hook.

**Front loop—front lp
Back loop— back lp**

Front Loop   Back Loop

**Front post stitch—fp:
Back post stitch—bp:** When working post st, insert hook from right to left around post st on previous row.

Back   Front

Post of
Stitch

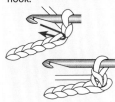

Half double crochet—hdc: Yo, insert hook in st, yo, pull through st, yo, pull through all 3 lps on hook.

Double crochet—dc: Yo, insert hook in st, yo, pull through st, [yo, pull through 2 lps] twice.

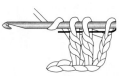

Change colors: Drop first color; with 2nd color, pull through last 2 lps of st.

Treble crochet—tr: Yo twice, insert hook in st, yo, pull through st, [yo, pull through 2 lps] 3 times.

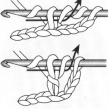

Double treble crochet—dtr: Yo 3 times, insert hook in st, yo, pull through st, [yo, pull through 2 lps], 4 times.

Single crochet decrease (sc dec): (Insert hook, yo, draw lp through) in each of the sts indicated, yo, draw through all lps on hook.

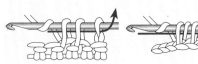

Example of 2-sc dec

Half double crochet decrease (hdc dec): (Yo, insert hook, yo, draw lp through) in each of the sts indicated, yo, draw through all lps on hook.

Example of 2-hdc dec

Double crochet decrease (dc dec): (Yo, insert hook, yo, draw loop through, draw through 2 lps on hook) in each of the sts indicated, yo, draw through all lps on hook.

Example of 2-dc dec

Treble crochet decrease (tr dec): Holding back last lp of each st, tr in each of the sts indicated, yo, pull through all lps on hook.

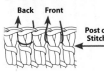

US	UK
sl st (slip stitch) =	sc (single crochet)
sc (single crochet) =	dc (double crochet)
hdc (half double crochet) =	htr (half treble crochet)
dc (double crochet) =	tr (treble crochet)
tr (treble crochet) =	dtr (double treble crochet)
dtr (double treble crochet) =	ttr (triple treble crochet)
skip =	miss